The Shyness Solution

CATHERINE GILLET, L.C.S.W.

Adamsmedia
Avon, Massachusetts

This book is dedicated to Dr. Samuel Klagsbrun,
whose guidance, warmth, humanity, and intelligence
has been an inspiration to many.

Published by
Adams Media,
a division of F+W Media, Inc.
57 Littlefield Street, Avon, MA 02322. U.S.A.
www.adamsmedia.com

ISBN 10: 1-4405-5868-X
ISBN 13: 978-1-4405-5868-9
eISBN 10: 1-4405-5869-8
eISBN 13: 978-1-4405-5869-6

Printed in the United States of America.

10 9 8 7 6 5 4 3 2 1

Previously published in 2005 under the title *The Shyness Solution* by Catherine Gillet, LCSW, copyright © F+W Media, Inc., ISBN 10: 1-59337-536-0;
ISBN 13: 978-1-59337-536-2.

*This book is available at quantity discounts for bulk purchases.
For information, please call 1-800-289-0963.*

contents

ACKNOWLEDGMENT TO YOU,
THE READER • iv

INTRODUCTION • v

 TOO SHY? • 1

 ONCE BITTEN, TWICE SHY • 13

SHY FOX • 21

SHY CHARM • 33

FUN SHY • 43

LOVE SHY • 57

 LIFE OF THE PARTY • 75

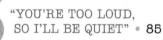 "YOU'RE TOO LOUD,
SO I'LL BE QUIET" • 85

PAINFULLY SHY • 103

PUTTING IT ALL TOGETHER • 109

APPENDIX A • 133

APPENDIX B • 137

APPENDIX C • 144

INDEX • 148

acknowledgment to you, the reader

66 Change has a considerable psychological impact on the human mind. To the fearful it is threatening because it means that things may get worse. To the hopeful it is encouraging because things may get better. To the confident it is inspiring because the challenge exists to make things better. 99

—*King Whitney Jr.*

Congratulations for choosing to embark on this journey of transforming your shyness into strength. As you practice the exercises in this book, you will solve your shyness. Give yourself a giant pat on the back for your determination and motivation. And remember, fear of failure is a natural and perfectly normal response when we venture into new territory. You have made a decision and choice to change your life for the better and you *will* succeed. You are not aiming for perfection here. The only thing required of you for success is a willingness to try. If you have a setback or disappointment, great! You've now joined the rest of the world. Every difficult situation you encounter is an opportunity for growth and greater self-awareness. It all depends on how you look at it. And now you are free to choose to look at your life in a hopeful, optimistic way. Once you have set the course of your life in a positive direction, there is no turning back. You now have nothing to lose besides your feelings of isolation, sadness, and pain. You are entitled to have the life you want. You deserve to be joyful and content with who you are. Living a rich, full, and meaningful existence is your birthright. Go for it!

introduction

"Our deepest fear is not that we are inadequate. Our deepest fear is that we are powerful beyond measure. It is our Light, not our Darkness, that most frightens us."

—*Marianne Williamson,*
A Return to Love, *1992*

The Shyness Solution is about transformation. It begins with acceptance of yourself as who you are and as you move through these pages, you will move toward a greater understanding and compassion for what you may have believed and experienced as a personal and social liability—shyness.

The journey toward self-acceptance and self-awareness is not easy. You will be challenged to rethink and deprogram shyness as stigma into shyness as strength.

If you are convinced that shyness is a negative trait which must be fought, conquered, defeated, and overcome, you will be asked to consider the positive aspects of this personality trait, of which there are many.

If you suffer from a diagnosed severe anxiety disorder, agoraphobia, and/or profound social phobia and fear resulting in debilitating panic attacks, you should seek the help of a professional trained in these disorders and then return to this book in the future.

The Shyness Solution is written for those of you who would like to dispel feelings of self-consciousness, inadequacy, and painful isolation from your lives. You will be asked to reconsider assumptions and negative self-definitions you may have held for years. The sojourn you will take may not be easy, but since the goal is a new attitude of self-compassion, enthusiasm, and hope, it will be well worth the time you spend. By listening to your inner wisdom and making friends with your shyness, you will be free to move in the world and your life with greater confidence and joy.

Through the exercises you will find in the following chapters, you will be assisted in identifying long-held beliefs about yourself and you will be given the tools to confront what is no longer working in your life and the encouragement you need to make a change.

As we embark on this journey of transformation, shyness will not be seen as a stigma to be ashamed of, but as a strength which can enrich your life and give you the courage to be yourself, fully, in any situation, social or otherwise. And you will be given practical assignments and advice on how to achieve your personal goal of finding a solution to your isolation and loneliness which your shyness may have contributed to.

As you follow the guidelines in this book you will find that acceptance will replace fear, positive affirmation will replace habitual negative self-image, and anxiety will be transformed into confidence.

Chapter One, *Too Shy?*, includes a questionnaire, which will help you rate your shyness level. You may be very surprised at the results!

Chapter Two, *Once Bitten, Twice Shy*, explores the ways in which past experiences and years of being labeled shy can be understood and solved with specific strategies designed to break the cycle of habitual shyness.

Chapter Three, *Shy Fox*, explores the healthy and productive aspects of shyness. Traits like tact, reserve, and modesty are valuable assets of the shy personality and are often overlooked in our Type A driven culture.

Chapter Four, *Shy Charm*, talks about other benefits of shyness, which can enhance your relationships with family, friends, and love interests. Among others, the techniques of "Thought Stopping" and "Acting as If," will be offered to assist you in transforming the manner in which you present yourself in the world of others.

Chapter Five, *Fun Shy*, offers other strategies aimed at developing the ability to enjoy the company of others. This chapter also includes tips to assist you in "The Art of Conversation" and how to feel less self-conscious when in a group or unfamiliar situation.

Chapter Six, *Love Shy*, delves into the mystery of attraction. You will learn why you may be reluctant to get involved in relationships, why they may be difficult to sustain, and finally, how to engage a love interest and feel safe while risking intimacy. It also offers specific locations and situations, which will assist you in expanding your social connections, circle of friends, and potential love interests.

Chapter Seven, *Life of the Party*, includes techniques for engaging in social situations comfortably and offers a new perspective on what it really means to be the "life" of any party or social gathering.

Chapter Eight, *You're Too Loud, So I'll Be Quiet,* discusses how what is termed "shyness" is often a reaction to the rhythms of a relationship or social dynamic where one many feel reluctant to assert themselves when surrounded by the non-shy. This chapter will also give you the understanding that you can choose who *you* wish to associate with and offers advice on types of people you may want to seek out, and types to avoid as you begin enlarging your social circle. This chapter also explores assertiveness versus aggression and how to ask for what you need and want from others in your relationships and career.

Chapter Nine, *Painfully Shy:* Along with offering advice such as seeking professional help, etc., for those who suffer from extreme social anxiety and phobia, this chapter also provides resources for support and connection with others who are on the same journey you are, as you continue your transformation from shy-fearful to shy-confident and strong.

Chapter Ten, *Putting It All Together* will use actual situations which elicit the fearful shy-response and walk you through specific instructions on how to use visualization and positive replacement of negative thoughts in order to conduct yourself with confidence and strength in the company of others.

Case studies of the following situations will be explored in depth using the five steps:

→ Going to a party and meeting new people.

→ Asking someone on a date.

→ Asserting yourself in the workplace.

→ Asking for what you need from friends.

→ Asking for what you need from family members.

→ Asking for what you need from a coworker.

→ Speaking in public.

CHAPTER ONE: ❝Don't fear failure so much that you refuse to try new things. The saddest summary of a life contains three descriptions: could have, might have, and should have.❞

—Louise E. Boone

Shyness as you've come to experience it has been painful and you may even have felt hopeless about the possibility of changing this aspect of your personality. The good news is that you will soon come to see yourself differently. Before we move ahead with the steps to transforming this externally imposed concept, which you have come to believe is your primary identity, it will be helpful for you to have a gauge of your shyness. It will assist in tailoring the exercises and suggestions to your personal style and comfort level. Chances are you have seen or taken lots of these types of quizzes.

Circle **A**, **B**, or **C** for the answer which reflects the way you are *most* likely to respond to the given situation. Your shyness quotient will be tallied at the end of the questionnaire.

RATE YOUR SHYNESS LEVEL

1. Do you feel nervous in situations where you will be meeting new people?
   a) Never
   b) Sometimes
   c) Always

2. Do you find yourself wishing you had more friends?
   a) Never
   b) Sometimes
   c) Always

3. You're walking down the street and you see a friend walking toward you with someone you don't know. Would you:
   a) Greet both and converse for a few minutes before saying goodbye and moving on.
   b) Wave as you walk by hurriedly, making it clear you have no intention of stopping.
   c) Duck into the closest store in order to avoid them.

4. Do you tend to feel most comfortable:
   a) With a few people you are close to

b) With one good friend

c) Alone

5. Which scenario sounds most inviting to you?
   a) Having a few people over to your place for an intimate dinner.
   b) Going out to a restaurant with one or two friends.
   c) Staying home and having dinner alone while you watch an old movie.

6. When you go to a party, are you the guest most likely to:
   a) Be one of the last to leave.
   b) Leave when most of the other guests do.
   c) Leave early.

7. You are on a long flight and the person next to you seems to obviously want to talk. Do you:
   a) Engage in the conversation.
   b) Talk for a while and then take out a book.
   c) Pretend you're asleep as soon as you fasten your seat belt.

8. You are sitting at an outdoor café with a couple of friends. They get into a heated argument. Do you:
   a) Remain in your seat even though you feel uncomfortable and wait for the argument to resolve.
   b) Attempt to change the subject, perhaps with humor.
   c) Excuse yourself and leave.

9. Do you tend to meet new people:
   a) On your own.
   b) Through friends.
   c) At work, church, or school.

10. As far as friends and acquaintances are concerned, would you say you have:
    a) A lot of friends and acquaintances.
    b) A few good friends and a lot of acquaintances.
    c) A few acquaintances and not many friends.

11. Your best friend knows you will be alone on Thanksgiving, so he invites you to spend the day with his extended family. Do you:
    a) Accept the invitation.
    b) Arrive in time for dinner and then leave as soon as it seems polite.
    c) Decline the invitation.

12. You meet someone you feel very comfortable around and you would like to be closer friends with her. She invites you to her beach house for the weekend along with several other people you have never met. Would you:
    a) Go for the weekend.
    b) Go for the day and not spend the night.
    c) Say you're sorry, but you have other plans.

13. When someone is angry with you for something you feel is unjustified, do you:
    a) Ask him/her to meet you for coffee so you can talk about it.

b) Wait a while, until he/she has had time to think about what happened and then call and talk on the phone.

c) Apologize even though you have done nothing wrong.

14. A person you are attracted to asks you on a date for the upcoming weekend. Do you:
   a) Accept even though you feel anxious about it.
   b) Tell him/her you are busy and ask if you can postpone until next weekend.
   c) Decline the offer because it makes you too nervous.

15. At a party, do you feel most comfortable:
   a) In the living room with everyone else.
   b) In the kitchen, helping the hostess with the food and drinks.
   c) Outside, playing fetch with the dog.

16. At the beginning of the semester, the instructor tells your class that an oral presentation will be required for completion of the course. Would you most likely:
   a) Give the presentation even though you are very nervous about it.
   b) Talk to your teacher about your fear of public speaking and ask if you can write an extra paper to satisfy the grade requirement.
   c) Drop the class without talking to the instructor.

17. It's your best friend's birthday and she's having a small dinner party comprised of people you've heard about, but have never met. Do you:
   a) Go to the party and try to have a good time for her sake.
   b) Arrange to take her out for lunch that day and skip the party.
   c) Call and tell her you have the flu.

18. You are walking on the treadmill at the gym and a very attractive member of the opposite sex on the treadmill next to you tries to strike up a conversation. Do you:
   a) Engage in the conversation.
   b) Smile politely, letting him/her know you are interested, talk for a few moments, and then excuse yourself.
   c) Say you're late for yoga class and hurry off.

19. Do you feel more at ease in:
   a) Large groups.
   b) Small groups.
   c) No group at all.

20. You've been shipwrecked on a deserted island. You can bring only one thing with you. Would it be:
   a) Your closest friend or intimate partner.
   b) Your dog (or cat).
   c) The entire collection of Harvard Classics.

21. You are out for dinner with a few friends or acquaintances. The person seated next to you talks with you and during the course of the conversation he says he senses you are shy. Do you:

a) Disagree, pointing to the fact that you are talking with him.

b) Ask him to clarify what he means by "shy"?

c) Agree with him and then feel self-conscious.

22. Your idea of a perfect evening with an intimate partner is:

a) Going out to eat followed by the movies with another couple before you head home alone together.

b) Spend a quiet evening with friends at your house or their place.

c) Order takeout and rent a movie and stay home with each other.

23. It's a beautiful, crisp Sunday in fall. Would you prefer to:

a) Call your closest friend and suggest he/she meets you for lunch and a walk in the park.

b) Stay home and e-mail friends and family to see how they're doing and let them know what you've been up to.

c) Go for a walk in the park by yourself and carry your portable CD player.

24. You were told by your boss you would be getting a raise in the New Year. It's now January and the paycheck in question arrives and you do not receive your raise, although coworkers have

gotten theirs. Are you more likely to:

a) Talk to your boss and ask what happened, before letting him/her know that you expect your raise immediately.

b) Ask a coworker to inquire for you about the status of your raise.

c) Say nothing.

25. A friend has done or said something that has hurt your feelings. Do you:

a) Express to your friend the manner in which he/she hurt you and say you'd like to resolve this issue.

b) Tell yourself it's no big deal and forget about it.

c) Stop talking to your friend without giving any reason.

26. You are upset with a partner or family member over something he/she has done that you feel was wrong. Would you:

a) Suggest a time when the two of you can sit down and talk about it.

b) Say nothing is wrong if he/she asks you if you are upset.

c) Tell yourself it's none of your business and you really don't have any right to be upset by his/her behavior.

27. A new love interest calls to cancel your date for that evening, saying he/she has to work late, and asks you out for another day. Are you most likely to:

a) Say you understand and ask what day he/she has in mind for rescheduling.

b) Tell him/her you are very busy yourself, so you'll call when your schedule clears later in the week to arrange another time.

c) Feel like he/she really doesn't want to see you and is making excuses, so you get off the phone as quickly as possible and do not return his/her calls.

28. There is an exhibition of your favorite artist at a large museum and you would really like to share the experience with another person. Would you:

a) Call a friend and ask if she'd like to join you.

b) Forward an e-mail about the show, saying this looks interesting and wait to see if she calls you to go along.

c) Contact no one and go alone.

29. Would you rather communicate with friends

a) In person.

b) On the telephone.

c) Via instant messaging or e-mail.

30. A close friend, who you haven't spoken to or seen for awhile since he moved to another part of the country, calls you. You hear his voice on the answering machine as you screen your calls. Do you usually:

a) Pick up the phone and talk to him.

b) Call him back later, hoping to get his machine,

but speak to him if he picks up the phone.

c) E-mail him, thanking him for his call and saying you're sorry you missed him.

If you answered mostly As (20 or more):

You might consider yourself shy, but you are aware of your strengths and you are not afraid to take risks that will enhance your relationships. You see yourself as capable of taking action despite any fear you may feel in a socially challenging situation. You may not call yourself extroverted by any means, but the manner in which you conduct yourself is with a great deal of courage and determination. You are willing to try to venture to dare to test your feelings of timidity in service to your goals and desires, which are important to you. You are committed to working hard to change the stigma of being labeled "shy" into a strength which will work in your best interest in order to achieve what you want most in life.

If you answered mostly Bs (15 or more):

You are on the brink of being able to transform your shyness into strength. You recognize that the self-defeating behavior of negative thinking is holding you back and you are trying to change and grow. You continue to feel uncomfortable in unfamiliar situations and you also tend to avoid confrontation, but you are moving forward to face your fears. You know you have your work cut out for you, but you are definitely up for the challenge and success is in your near future.

If you answered mostly Cs (20 or more):

You are really trying to undo years of habitual labeling. You have a strong desire to change and broaden your life to include others, but since you have difficulty trusting, this is not an easy task for you. You may have been deeply hurt in the past and feel safe and secure only when you are alone. You want to change this pattern however, and you are willing to try to face your fears. All you need now is a willingness to try. The exercises in this book will be particularly helpful for you as you initiate this positive transformation in your life. You will need to proceed slowly, and feel free to amend the exercises to suit your comfort level so you have the highest chance for success.

CHAPTER TWO: "Look not mournfully into the past. It comes not back again. Wisely improve the present. It is thine. Go forth and meet the future, without fear…"
—*Henry Wadsworth Longfellow (1807–1882)*

Is shyness innate or learned? Much research has been devoted to the subject of nature vs. nurture regarding temperament. Mothers describe their babies as "easy," "difficult," "timid," or "fearless." Introversion and extroversion have been documented as inherent characteristics in infants.

So, perhaps you arrived in the world, predisposed to being shy. Or maybe you learned to be shy due to the nature of your family or cultural environment. There's no question, regardless of the origin, once you have been labeled "shy," it tends to become a personality description that is not easy to alter.

Jim, thirty years old, speaks of his upbringing in a large, extended family:

"I divide my family into 'hollerers' and 'screechers.' We're Italian and any holiday or family gathering included at least a hundred people, all of them talking and laughing louder than the next. The 'hollerers' tended to be the ones who seemed to like to carry on a conversation with someone on the other side of the room. The 'screechers' could be standing a foot away, but I guess they didn't think you could hear them unless they yelled in your face. They weren't angry or anything. Just very demonstrative and loud—very loud. Even in small groups. I can't remember my family ever having a normal, remotely quiet conversation. It's like they got stuck on one volume level, ten, and had no idea how to communicate at a two or three. I spent a lot of time in my room with the headphones on listening to folk music. Everyone said I was shy, but I just couldn't stand all the noise. I got so good at being alone, it started being uncomfortable for me to be around people. Not just my family, but anybody. I liked being alone because I was used to it. I felt calmer in my own world."

There are many childhood environmental factors that can contribute to the development of a "shy" personality. A chaotic household; early trauma such as illness, accident, or loss of a parent; an emotionally unstable caretaker; peer teasing; frequent relocation; or academic difficulties can contribute to some people developing a more timid approach when they needed to interact with others. In most of these scenarios, trust is the underlying issue.

People who identify themselves as shy often cite trust as a major problem. They either have little trust in others, or place too much trust in people, which eventually leads to disappointment and a self-perpetuating cycle of hurt. We all desire to belong to a group, to have close relationships with others. Shy people often feel excluded from their right to attain this basic human need.

We can even develop a fear of intimacy, of getting too close to someone due to our experiences because we dread that intimacy with another will only lead to abandonment and rejection and loss. The shy person then shies away from social contact because he or she anticipates a negative outcome of hurt and betrayal of trust.

In any relationship, it's important to have healthy boundaries. Trusting indiscriminately or placing too much trust in someone before they have demonstrated trustworthiness sets the stage for feeling frustrated, let down, and wounded.

But the answer doesn't rest in isolation to avoid being hurt. Many shy people report feeling more comfortable when they are alone. No one can hurt us if we are alone. But as any person who experiences shyness can tell you, isolation doesn't eliminate pain. It creates a different kind of pain—loneliness.

Shyness can actually be a great motivator to developing healthy intimacy. The need for clear boundaries has already been established. Having spent much time alone, you are comfortable with yourself. Do you know how lucky that makes you? Many people have great difficulty with solitude.

This is one of the gifts of shyness. One becomes more aware of themselves and the pain you feel in separation from others is what can spur you into taking a risk to allow intimacy into your life.

Not that this is an easy task. Solitude can become a way of life for some. The comfort/safety zone of detachment is measured against the uncomfortable feeling of being with others and we can then hightail it back to our cozy dens of seclusion.

If you're reading this book, you know on some level that this is no way to live. Choosing solitude out of fear is a very painful way to exist in the world. In order to do this you must cut off many of your feelings. The primary one being your desire to feel the joy and enthusiasm that comes from living a full and balanced life.

If you feel that your shyness stems from something in your past, you are fortunate. You can begin to understand that your feelings of isolation and loneliness have been externally imposed upon you and you are free to choose to make a choice about whether or not shyness is hindering you in your desires and goals.

It will be helpful at this point to get out a notebook and write:

→ A timeline of your life from your earliest memories to the present time. Include both negative and positive.

→ A short, personalized bio of all members of your nuclear family. (Personalized here means your impressions of them.)

➡️ What are your family's predominant personality traits?

➡️ When you were growing up, what was important to them in terms of how they related to you?

➡️ How did you feel you needed to "be" around them?

➡️ How do you feel each of them saw you as you aged?

Now look at your list and underline any event, circumstance, personality trait, relationship, or interpersonal dynamic that you feel might have contributed to your developing a shy approach to the world. Was your father fearful and a "worrier"? Was your mother obsessed with outer success and achievement? Was your older brother the shining star you couldn't match? These observations are not the definitive answer to the reason why you became identified as shy, but it is helpful to trace back to the origins of where our beliefs were formed in order to change them.

Should you realize that the origin lies in some past trauma, you may want to seek out a therapist to talk with or join a group comprised of others like you who are attempting to live more fully in the world. Therapeutic assistance can be very helpful in facilitating understanding of the nature of your fear so you can heal and move on to pursue your aspirations. A resource directory of Web sites and literature is included later on in this book.

For most, shyness has become a habitual, reflexive way of "being" in the world. You can choose to end the self-defeating aspects of this behavior. Years of being labeled "shy" and the subsequent beliefs you have adopted about yourself can be redefined and changed. But all change requires courage. Courage requires motivation, and if you are motivated, you can release yourself from the bondage of a label imposed on you that is holding you emotionally hostage. Your negative assumptions about yourself and your view of shyness as a stigma will keep you from interacting from a place of joy and will dis-empower you from shining your unique, beautiful spirit in the world. If you are motivated, you will succeed. Anything worth it is difficult, but feeling fully alive and vibrant, self-confident and whole, is well worth the effort required.

WE ARE WHAT WE BELIEVE

If you think that shyness is a liability, a cross you have to bear and are feeling hopeless about ever "fitting in," think again. Our beliefs are formed early in life—some of them positive, and some negative. Beliefs can be changed. They are simply a construct that we have come to hold as truth. There is nothing more defeating and debilitating than to repetitively engage in behaviors that bring painful results over and over again.

So it is with a belief system which no longer works for you. In order to change your attitude about shyness you first must understand how it has served you.

> Write a list of the ways, both negative and positive, in which shyness has been an important part of your life.

Using words like "overcoming," "defeating," "conquering," and "eradicating," when describing transforming shyness will keep you on a treadmill of recycled pain. These words imply there is something wrong with you—which there is definitely not! (Statistics cite that more than 50 percent of the population describe themselves as shy to varying degrees.) The assumption that shyness is a foe that must be vanquished misses the point entirely and, like trying to extricate yourself from quicksand, the more you struggle to remove shyness from your identity and experience, the higher the chances of failure, which only reinforces your hopelessness about the possibility of change.

What is needed is a complete and radical redefinition of what it means to be shy. In *The Shyness Solution*, shyness will be viewed as strength, and we will use the term shy-strength. Once you accept shyness as a part of you, you can choose which aspects you'd like to keep and discard those that are no longer promoting growth and optimism for the future.

You are a multifaceted being. In other words, there are many parts of you. Shyness is just one of them. Your desire to feel more connected to the world is another, equally strong aspect of your self. The need for security and safety is extremely important when exploring letting go of the aspects of shyness that are holding you back from your dreams. This will be clear when we reach the exercises and practices designed to assist you as you move toward having greater confidence in your interactions with the world. After years of avoidance, you can't expect yourself to leap into social situations with the greatest of ease. Your need for safety must be honored, and this will be achieved with small steps and lots of practice in environments and with people you feel comfortable around.

Our egos are designed to maintain the status quo and to resist anything that threatens this: i.e., change. Any change is a threat to the identity we have constructed and come to believe is who we are. Even if it is for growth and greater well-being, a part of us will be resistant to transformation. This is where courage comes in. And the will to create a different mode of interaction with ourselves and others. The only battle you will engage in is with the habitual negative thinking which is keeping you stuck. The parts of you that want to live a rich, full, and rewarding life have been waiting a long time for their day in the sun. It's time now to listen to them and give as much energy to the belief that you can be shy and live the life you desire, as you have given the belief that shyness is a curse you must endure. We are what we believe. And you have the ability to freely choose what you believe about yourself.

CHAPTER THREE: 66To use fear as the friend it is, we must retrain and reprogram ourselves. We must persistently and convincingly tell ourselves that the fear is here—with its gift of energy and heightened awareness—so we can do our best and learn the most in the new situation.99

—*Peter McWilliams,* Life 101

This chapter is devoted to uncovering the healthy, life-affirming aspects of being shy. There are many benefits to the trait of shyness. Having spent much of your life believing shyness is anything but an asset, you may find it difficult to accept that this part of your personality is actually positive and useful.

The negative view of shyness is repeatedly reinforced by societal values. Culturally, we have come to place high value on extroverted traits such as ambitious assertiveness. It has been documented that people who describe themselves as shy tend to be passed over for promotions in the workplace.

Let's face it. We live in a "Type A"–driven society, where the squeaky wheel seems to always reap the highest rewards. Aggressive posturing and intimidation have come to be accepted as normal business practice. We can all think of a boss, coworker, acquaintance, or friend, who through an overbearing, aggressively self-promoting attitude not only maintains their position, but frequently are rewarded with advancement.

What is a shy person to do? You can't change yourself into an ambition-obsessed, aggressively self-assured extrovert, and why would you even want to?

The goal here is not to act like the Romans just because you find yourself in a Rome full of gladiators, but in finding a way to navigate social situations including your career, without succumbing to external pressure to be someone you're not.

If you believe that only aggressively assertive, non-shy people succeed in relationships and at work, this belief must be challenged with the facts.

Shyness by its nature carries with it some remarkable qualities. The personal assets you possess are far more valuable in the real sense of what it means to be a moral, decent human being, which is ultimately the measure of true success.

Make a list of personality traits you admire. Make a list of personality traits you dislike. Highlight or check off the ones you believe you possess.

GENTLENESS

Shy people are often described as very gentle, especially when it comes to dealing with others. Much of the literature on shyness focuses on the shy person's inability to say "no," their need for approval, and fear of rejection as the source of their increased empathy.

All of these are negative assumptions about the origin of a wonderful strength and gift: compassion. Since it is undervalued in our outer success-driven culture, gentleness is often viewed as weakness. If you buy into this type of thinking you will remain feeling powerless. You will assume the outer negative identification and believe that because you are kind, you are fearful and weak. Nothing could be further from the truth.

You can choose to transform this old idea of gentility as weakness into the belief that it is an essential strength you are fortunate to possess. Compassion for others and for ourselves is a tremendous asset and source of energy which draws people to you. All it takes is a shift in your belief system. Whenever you think "fear," replace it with "strength." If you think "weakness," remind yourself that this is an externally imposed idea that you are choosing to reject.

As mentioned, this type of transformation requires a great deal of courage, another quality that you have in abundance. A shy person living in this world is constantly being asked to overcome their fear. Taking risks in spite of your fear is your daily routine, and is the definition of true courage.

You may think, *All I want to do is fit in and feel like everyone else*. Truth be known, everyone is insecure about something. Without fear, we would never even have survived as a species. Everyone is fearful of one thing or another. To swim upstream against the current of popular assumptions and redefine them in order to find your place of strength, requires you to be independent and brave. And guess what? If you are shy, you are extremely independent. No one knows what it's like to have the responsibility for themselves and their thoughts, painful as they may be, as those who intimately know shyness. Years of longing to belong to the group have made you aware of the painfulness of separation. Through solitude you have come to know yourself, what you may feel you have been missing out on and subsequently, what you want your life to look and feel like. You can change the traditionally held belief of solitude as loneliness into solitude as the way you have forged an independent spirit. Nothing is more frightening to most people than solitude. In fact, lots of extroverts became that way because they could not tolerate the feeling of being alone. It takes a great deal of courage to sit with oneself and examine one's fears. Congratulations. You've done the hard work, now you can take this independent strength into the world.

AFFIRMATION: "My shyness and time alone has taught me to be a kind, generous, compassionate, and gentle human being."

MODESTY

"Never over-, under-, or misrepresent yourself." Shy people tend to be cautious when it comes to self-aggrandizement, so they follow that mantra. What a wonderful trait to possess! Boasting and bragging are not part of your repertoire of social interactivity.

This is a very appealing quality, which again can draw others to you as long as you believe it to be what it truly is: a phenomenal strength. Flagrant self-promotion is not something a shy person engages in. There are ways you can promote yourself using your own personal style and shy-strength, which we will discuss later. For now we are talking about personal hype and the types of behaviors which are expected and to a certain extent, accepted by the majority as a sign of self-esteem. This is very much an emperor in his new clothes phenomena, as most people abhor a shameless self-promoter, but these behaviors are not only tolerated and emulated, but rewarded in certain situations. The one area where it is definitely not valued is in interpersonal relationships.

Modesty is a strength admired by all. Think of the person who has attained great achievements in life (and these don't have to be fame and fortune related) and have retained a sense of modesty. These are the people we tend to truly admire. Achieving success while keeping one's modesty intact is not an easy task in the current world. Transform your thinking now about your "inability" to be aggressively self-promoting. Modesty is a quiet strength that the shy inherently possess. It is another outcome of the gift of shyness.

TACT AND RESERVE

Our senses are currently assaulted daily with tell-all, spill-all, reality-obsessed entertainment which insults the spirit, especially the spirits of sensitive souls out there, like yourselves. For you, the phrase "fear-factor" relates more to fearing the lengths some people will go to degrade themselves.

Tact and reserve are strengths that naturally reside in the realm of the shy. You can now begin to review your reluctance to enter into a heated and hurtful conversation as evidence of your ability to employ tact. So it also goes for harmful gossip and slander. These types of pursuits don't interest you, not because, as you may have formerly believed, you can't think of anything to say, but rather, you have no desire to participate in something which is destructive and painful to others.

Reserve and tactfulness are benefits of shyness which our present culture has deprived itself of. Be grateful for this gift.

Deborah described meeting a man who made a lasting impression on her at a dinner party once, and who radically changed her view of shyness. She said she first noticed him the moment she walked into the room because of his confident stature and manner in which he was dressed. He was very well groomed and elegantly attired. She said she soon forgot about him however, because he spoke to no one. She had even forgotten he was there when they were all seated for dinner. He took his place and smiled politely, but did not engage in the chitchat of the dinner conversation. She remarked that he seemed friendly and not aloof or snobbish, just very shy and quiet. He laughed at the other's jokes and nodded in agreement about the excellence of the food being served.

Deborah herself, being a reformed habitually shy person, felt she knew a fellow "sufferer." The other guests ignored him and no one tried to engage him in conversation or ask him questions about himself. She said it was like he was invisible. At a certain point, the topic of conversation turned to the merits or lack of merit in the current art world. After several minutes of a heated discussion around the table, the "shy" man spoke. All eyes turned in his direction. There was a hushed silence at the table as this man spoke both eloquently and with great intelligence on the subject, offering several perspectives and possibilities for further discussion. It was then that Deborah realized that what had appeared as painful shyness was really a quiet strength. The man was perfectly comfortable being at the party, being himself and speaking when he felt moved to do so. She mentioned feeling a sense of awe that someone could be so comfortable with themselves and their shyness that it actually made him come across as someone with a great deal of depth of character.

This man knew how to transform his shyness into shy-strength. Comfortable with himself, he was able to present himself in a social situation without feeling inadequate or nervous that his quiet demeanor would be judged negatively by others. He trusted that when he felt the need or desire to speak, he would.

AFFIRMATION: "I honor my tactfulness and reserve as shy-strengths and I am grateful for them."

INSECURITY

Healthy self-esteem is often defined as the lack of insecurity. But in fact, self-esteem has nothing to do with security. Self-esteem is the ability to place value in ourselves by accepting all parts of who we are, flaws and all.

Perfectionism is the enemy of self-esteem. Many shy people report feeling they need to be perfect in order to be accepted by others. Talk about setting yourself up for failure! Ask yourself if you would like to associate with only "perfect" people. Your answer should give you some indication of why you need to let go of the idea of perfection for yourself as the only way you will have friends, do well at your job, or find/keep a partner.

Our insecurities can teach us much about ourselves. In fact, they are very often the impetus to change and transformation.

> Make a list of people, things, and situations that make you feel insecure. Differentiate between things that make you feel shy. For example: "When I call a friend and he doesn't call me back" is an insecurity-producing situation, not one that automatically elicits the shy response.

Alan Watts, a Zen teacher and writer, spoke of the "wisdom of insecurity." Viewed in this way, our insecurities are our teachers and the lessons taught are powerful guides toward achieving self-confidence and awareness.

If we felt terrific all the time, content with ourselves and perfectly happy with how we relate to others and the world at large, there would be no reason to change. And when nothing changes, nothing grows.

Our insecurities help us redefine who we are, what we want, and give us the motivation necessary to implement these desires. Questioning ourselves is healthy. As long as it does not veer into the judgmental and harsh.

Nothing is guaranteed in life. Insecurity is inherent in our existence. Shy people understand this and sense the vulnerability and fragility of life, because they feel it within themselves. Insecurity is transformed into a shy-strength by acknowledging your gift of awareness of the preciousness of our limited time here. It's why you want so dearly to make the most of it, and to feel connected to others. Insecurity is a liability when we take on the negativity of an emotion and make it a fact about ourselves that we then place belief in.

Most of us would feel uneasy if we reached out to someone and the person did not return our call. The negative, insecure thoughts might be: "He doesn't really like me, he probably thinks I'm a pest, he doesn't want to talk me because I'm so boring," etc., etc.

The technique of "Thought Stopping" is especially important and helpful when our negative, judgmental voice begins to whisper incessantly in our ear, making us feel powerless and ashamed. (Tools for learning Thought Stopping will follow in the next chapter.)

The difference between understanding insecurity as strength and getting stuck in negative insecurity is fear. Fear is the drive behind negative thought processes. It makes us react in ways we would not if we were in a centered place of security and confidence. When we react out of fear we cause problems for ourselves, the most common being feelings of regret and shame. Our fears may make us second-guess our decisions and convince us that a situation could have been handled better when we actually may have handled it very well.

For instance, take the same scenario: You call a friend and he doesn't call you back. Instead of going through the self-destructive rant, which may only fill you with dread and self-pity, stop the negative thoughts and *will* yourself to think positive ones. Replace every negative thought with a positive one. This is the battle mentioned earlier. A positive thought replacement would be, "I know my friend cares about me. And my calling shows I care about him. I know he's been very busy lately. He'll call back when he has the time. And if I don't hear from him in a few days, I'll call him back and ask how he's doing and if he's okay."

Practice this type of thought replacement every time your mind wants to react from a fearful place. Practice being mindful of your thinking. Observe when you are more prone to negative fear-based thinking. These are the areas you will want to work with. With practice you will be able to identify and eventually anticipate the type of scenarios which are particularly insecurity-producing for you. Once you have identified the feeling you can choose to react in a less self-injurious manner.

Say you are sitting with a couple of friends who are chatting away. You begin to feel anxious, fearful you will have nothing to contribute to the conversation. The negative voice may sound something like this: "I can't think of anything to say." (Fearful reaction.) "I should just leave before they notice how pathetic I am." Interpret insecurity here—the need to be perfect, and replace it with a positive interpretation: "I am really enjoying sitting here in this outdoor café on a beautiful day with my friends. I am a good listener and they appreciate that about me."

AFFIRMATION: "My insecurities are my teachers. They are how I learn about myself. My insecurity has taught me that life and relationships are precious and valuable."

SENSITIVITY

How many shy people have heard the statement: "You're so sensitive," or "She's very sensitive" and then attributed a negative connotation to it? Sensitivity is another shy-strength that must be redefined if we are to embrace it as a unique and wonderful quality.

Shy people do tend to be more sensitive. By sensitive we mean empathic and compassionate. You are more sensitive to the feelings of others. Having spent a lot of time with yourself and your own thoughts, you have created a way of observing the world that is highly attuned to many things others do not notice. Your gift of intuition is very strong. When you feel it is with intensity. Joy, fear, sadness, happiness, when you feel something, you really feel it! Practice sharing how you feel with others. Notice what keeps you from being able to do this. Is it fear? Fear of what? Judgment? Failure? Embarrassment?

Your sensitive nature is another reason why people will be drawn to you if you challenge yourself to express this quality with openness and honesty. You feel strongly about many things. You have an opportunity to share these beliefs and feelings with others and they will be grateful for it. Practice with people you feel most comfortable around. Tell them you'd like to talk about something you feel passionate about. Being a sensitive being has also given you a generosity of spirit, something

which you have a right, opportunity, and in many ways, a
wonderful obligation to share.

AFFIRMATION: "I am a sensitive person. I feel things deeply. I want to share this part of myself with others."

Make a list of things you feel strongly about, things that
are important to you, and things you believe in.

CHAPTER FOUR: "For the most part, fear is nothing but an illusion. When you share it with someone else, it tends to disappear."

—*Marilyn C. Barrick*

As if modesty, tact, reserve, compassion, sensitivity, self-understanding, the ability to feel comfortable alone, and generosity of spirit weren't enough, there is also a mysterious aura that emanates from the shy-strong person.

Once you have begun the journey of transforming your shyness into strength, and you gain confidence in yourself around other people, you will experience a new phenomenon. You are irresistibly charming! By embracing your shyness as a part of who you are (and not the entirety), you will then be better able to allow other parts of yourself to emerge. The playful, the child-like, and the wise and perhaps eccentric aspects of your personality will no longer be suppressed out of fear of rejection or shame.

Viewing your shyness as strength helps you act "as if" in any situation. All of the beautiful qualities you have been hiding can now be brought into the world. Others are drawn to the shy-strong because they exhibit personality traits and attributes of true strength.

As mentioned, the ability to feel comfortable alone is a rare gift. Once you have redefined "social phobia" as a kind of courage, which being able to tolerate solitude requires, you will project this confidence in your dealings with others in the world of relationships, family, and the workplace.

By accepting your shyness as a part of you, you are saying in effect, "I don't need you to be okay with me, but I will choose to be with you because I enjoy your company and being around you makes me feel good about myself."

Your quiet demeanor, humor, humility about yourself in the face of your fears, and listening skills and interest in others, makes you attractive and desirable. The phrase "still waters run deep" aptly applies to shy-strong people. Your natural intuition when it comes to others will help you make astute observations as to what they need in a given situation, and will assist you in responding accordingly.

Shy-strong people are great observers of human nature because they have had plenty of practice observing their own. Combine this with sharp listening skills and you've got the one-two combo which all surveys state as the most attractive trait in a partner or friend: someone who listens and someone who is sensitive and nonjudgmental regarding needs and feelings.

As we have learned, one of the basic needs for all human beings is safety and security. The shy-strong individual has a very personal reference to this basic need, since it is the one that has motivated your desire for transformation. Being extremely mindful of this need for your *own* comfort, you naturally try to ensure it for others. You create a safe haven for others to express themselves without fear of prejudice or criticism.

Another reason people are drawn to the shy-strong is that they are very easy to be around. Prior to transforming your shyness into strength, this was probably not the case. The non-shy are often uncomfortable around the intensely insecure person. In one study, when an extrovert and introvert were placed in a room together, the extrovert eventually became introverted since without verbal interaction he became confused about his identity and felt lost. This illustrates how strong a pull negatively shy behavior can exert.

If we transform shy into shy-strength, we have a real power in our possession. So yes, the non-shy may feel uncomfortable and at a "loss for words" around the timid. But they are mesmerized by the shy-strong. This is due to the fact that the charm of the shy-strong person lies in their embodiment of many qualities which are underdeveloped in the extrovert, who has perhaps spent little time alone, or getting to know himself and his motivations intimately.

The shy-strong are also irresistible to the still painfully shy and you can be a wonderful role model for your friends who are continuing to experience difficulty with being labeled "shy" as you stay true to your positive nature and practice redefining what it means to be shy by your actions and words.

So use that charm! Go ahead and even flirt in your quiet, modest way. Talk in your soft tone. Continue your hesitancy to brag and gossip. Use your innate diplomacy and tact when it is called for and above all, express your passion for life, which all who meet you will see, find alluring and therefore, wish to get to know more about you.

THOUGHT STOPPING

Choosing to replace a negative thought with a positive one requires the use of the technique of "Thought Stopping." Habitual negative thinking is second nature to most of us. When our insecurities are triggered, we go into an automatic response of interpreting whatever provoked the insecurity. For example, we may think no one wants to talk to us at a party. The negative thoughts start to roll: "I am boring and everyone knows it. They can tell I am uninteresting and not worth talking to" . . . until we create the avalanche of reacting out of fear and probably leaving the party, feeling hopeless and defeated.

The technique of Thought Stopping works like this: A negative thought arises and you literally close the door on it. You will need to actually imagine a door. The doors can be made of anything you choose, carved mahogany, two-foot thick steel, marble, a velvet curtain—anything you feel will be most effective in keeping the self-defeating thoughts securely banished from your desire and willingness to create a positive attitude.

Once you have stopped the negativity from dominating your thinking, you are free to choose a more positive thought/interpretation: "I don't know many people here, so of course they are not going to just come up to me. After all, I am not going up to them. I'll find someone here I know and sit with that person until I feel more comfortable."

Thought Stopping is not only useful in actual "live" experiences, but can be beneficial in many areas. Having negative thoughts about ourselves is one of the ways we keep ourselves imprisoned in isolation. It is almost impossible to entertain the possibility that others find us attractive, intelligent, interesting, and fun to be with if we don't believe these are qualities we possess.

If you can master the technique of stopping negative thoughts, you will be able to transform yourself into the person you truly are and desire to be. You can change the old ingrained habit of regarding yourself as "less than" into the positive belief that you have much to offer.

It's an "inside job" as they say, and before you can trust and believe that other people enjoy your company, you must first learn to delight in your own being. For an old habit to change, there must first be the recognition that it is something which is not only no longer serving you, but is actually deterring you from the type of life and connection to others you long for. Once you have made the commitment to change, like with any habit, you must call upon your will-power to assist you in manifesting this transformation.

Negative thinking about oneself is not easy to ignore. These self-defeating thoughts have the power of years invested in them. And you may find replacing the negative with the positive a daunting task. But the more you practice this, the easier it will be to "talk back" to self-defeating thoughts.

ACTING AS IF

Another tool you can use to assist your negative Thought Stopping is "Acting as If." Suppose you are nervous about speaking before a group. The first task here is to be knowledgeable and confident in the material you are about to present. When you Act as If, you actually take on the role you would like to present yourself as. If you would like to Act as If . . ."I am confident and in control in this situation," you would then imagine yourself in front of a group, delivering your speech with clarity and command.

Acting as If, as it is used here, is precisely that. You play a part or role. You consciously choose to step outside yourself for the time being and adopt the persona you desire to convey, in order to achieve your goals.

This technique can be used in any situation. You can Act as If . . . "I am happy to be at this dinner party." You can Act as If . . . "I believe I am interesting and engaging company."

Acting as If is most helpful in the early stages of the Thought Stopping practice and you may want to combine the two techniques. As you train your mind to shift from negative to positive thinking you may find it helpful to choose to act in a positive and different way. This technique, although sometimes difficult for the extremely shy, is an excellent way to accelerate your mind's acceptance of the transformation from shy to shy-strong that you are committed to achieving.

Acting as If does not mean you are going to be portraying or will be perceived as a phony or poser. It simply means you are "trying on" the personality you wish to ultimately project when in the company of others and in specific situations.

Acting as If can be great fun if you approach it lightheartedly. Practice by starting out with simple tasks. For example, go into your favorite coffee shop and Act as If you had just won the lottery. You are in a wonderful mood. You convey this positive energy to the waiter or maybe someone else who is waiting, by smiling and saying hello and perhaps even remarking on the weather. Experience yourself in a familiar social situation with an upbeat, positive attitude. This may be an attitude you have had difficulty feeling about yourself in the past. Try it out and see if you don't walk back out onto the sidewalk with a spring in your step, and a feeling of renewed enthusiasm. You were able to do something differently, and these small steps will lead to the confidence you are building upon in order to engage in situations which have in the past been laden with fear and the feeling of being an uncomfortable outsider.

Karen speaks of Acting as If in the following way:

"At first I was reluctant to try to act like anyone other than who I am. I have been shy all my life and I was afraid my friends would think I had gone crazy if I all of a sudden started being outgoing. I got the courage to try it when something important happened.

My brother really wanted me to speak at his wedding. We are twins and we've always been very close. He's my best friend. There were so many things I wanted to say, to show up for him, to let everyone know how special he is and how much he means to me and how happy I was for him. I wanted to maybe even tell a joke that he would appreciate and would let his new family know what a great sense of humor he has. We always had so much fun together and there were stories about crazy things we had done, which he of course initiated, that I knew he would appreciate. I also knew how important it was for him for me to get up there and say something. He was always an inspiration to me and I so wanted to do this for him, but the thought of standing in front of 200 people was terrifying to me. But the thought of disappointing him made me feel worse, so I told myself this isn't about me. It's about my brother and the happiest day of his life and I'm going to get up there and get out of my own way and Act as If I am not frightened because if I had walked out of that hall after the reception and didn't have the nerve to honor him, I would have regretted it forever. So I did it. I was shaking, but I kept telling myself I could do it and I could act for ten minutes like someone who wasn't afraid and forget about me and my fears and pretend I was strong—for him.

I am so grateful I did not only for my brother, but for me. I actually felt strong while I was up there acting strong. People came up to me and said wonderful things afterward which of course made me feel great, but the best part was when my brother came up and gave me a big hug and told me how proud he was that I was his sister and friend."

Acting as If does not have to be used only in situations like Karen's. But the important part of her story and the lesson for us here is her desire. Her want to honor and "show up" for her brother was stronger than her fear of talking to a room full of people she didn't know. As she said, she had to get out of her own way, which we can translate as not giving into habitual negative self-consciousness. She consciously chose to act in the manner in which she wished to be perceived. She did not let her fear control her, but rather she controlled her fear. This is one of the crucial points in learning to transform shyness into strength. Instead of allowing our fear to run our lives and make us run away from experiences we desperately wish to be part of, we can, with conscious effort, make the choice to take a risk. It is very important to remember that fear is an emotion, and any emotion can be tamed if we bring in a strong desire to take positive action, in spite of our fear.

fun shy

CHAPTER FIVE: "Do not be too timid and squeamish about your actions. All life is an experiment. The more experiments you make the better. What if they are a little coarse, and you may get your coat soiled or torn? What if you do fail, and get fairly rolled in the dirt once or twice. Up again, you shall never be so afraid of a tumble."

—*Ralph Waldo Emerson*

How many times have you said to yourself, "I wish I could enjoy myself around other people"? Even though these two statements come from different desires—wanting to *be* more fun is not the same as wanting to *have* more fun, they both stem from the same origin: self-consciousness.

This chapter is devoted to helping you rid yourself of the hyperawareness of yourself that keeps you from fully engaging in social interactions and situations.

Bob describes self-consciousness in the following way:

"Whenever I'm around other people, it's like I sit there and watch myself from the back of my head. I'm constantly thinking about what I say or don't say, how I'm sitting or standing and how the other people might interpret that, or judge me. But I know I'm constantly judging myself. It's like I'm analyzing so much in my own head I can't even hear the conversation, let alone participate. I always come home exhausted and worn out and feeling like an idiot. I've tried having a couple of drinks at a party, to loosen up and shut my head up, but I found drinking makes it worse because then I have to worry if I'm making an extra fool of myself. I dread parties or get-togethers and I'll find any excuse not to go because I know I won't have fun and I'll just beat myself up later, going through every thing I said (or didn't say) and thinking I was boring or stupid."

It's no wonder Bob has trouble enjoying himself in the company of others. As he said, he spends most of the time filled with self-doubt and fear that he will be judged harshly by the people he is with. We can learn a big lesson from Bob. Being Fun-Shy is really just being afraid to let down your guard (the judgmental, negative voice we spoke of earlier) and allowing yourself to be present in the moment.

Buddhist philosophy teaches us that all suffering comes from being unable to experience the present moment. To live in the past or the future and allow our minds to dictate how we feel is counterproductive to feelings of happiness.

THOUGHT NAMING

A technique that is particularly helpful here is Thought Naming. This entails precisely what it says: naming your thoughts. As you get comfortable with this technique, you will be able to employ it in social situations. But first it will be helpful to get to know your own mind and the particular ways you allow your thoughts to inform your actions.

Meditation is a wonderful tool to help you understand and quiet your mind. If you want to study formal meditation or join a meditation group, great! But for now, all you need is ten minutes a day:

- Sit in a quiet place, in a comfortable position, but not so comfortable that you fall asleep.

- Close your eyes.

- Focus on your breathing.

- You will know you are breathing correctly if, when you put your hand on your abdomen as you breathe in, your stomach rises, as you breathe out, it contracts.

- Breathe slowly, comfortably, and rhythmically.

- Just focus on the in and out of your breath.

- Let your mind quiet down.

- As thoughts arise, notice them and let them go.

- Do not judge any thoughts that come up.

- Just notice them, and then return to your breathing.

→ If any thought becomes too intense, continue your breathing, focusing on the in and out of your breath. You will see that the thought will change and your mind will move on to another one.

→ Whenever you find yourself "thinking," simply return to focusing on your breath.

Training the mind in this way will help you as we take this practice deeper and into the world of others. For example, say you are with a group of people. You've been doing your daily ten minutes of meditation, watching your mind and how it generates all sorts of thoughts. You are beginning to quiet down the observer in your head. You will know this is happening if either he or she has been less "vocal" or you are able to "catch" it in the act of harsh judgmental criticism. Now you are going to add something here. You can now begin to name your thoughts.

For a variety of reasons, most of us do not spend our times thinking loving, compassionate, and kind thoughts about ourselves. When we do think about ourselves, it is usually in terms of what we lack and so we then focus on our deficiencies instead of our strengths. We tend to dwell on what we are not doing instead of what we have accomplished, what we are not instead of what we are. All of this self-assessment is viewed through the lens of negativity and judgment. We compare ourselves to others, feeling they are somehow better than we are. We worry what others will think of us. We tend to be very hard on ourselves and this is directly connected to negative thoughts. This vicious cycle of self-defeating thinking can be changed.

By naming your thoughts, you will be confronting your own negative thinking and defusing these self-esteem bombs by recognizing them for what they are. For our purposes, negative thinking falls into three categories: Fear, Irrationality, and Bad Habit.

The acronym F.I.B. is a good one, since these negative thoughts are actually false assumptions you have believed about yourself for some time. Here is an example of how this type of thinking works. Notice the crescendo that these thoughts can reach. Once you have given in to fear-based thinking, your mind will keep going until you convince yourself you are not capable of success.

Say you must give a presentation at your job in front of several people, including the CEO of your company. The following thoughts may arise:

- **FEAR:** "There is no way I can do this. If I try to give this presentation, especially in front of everyone at my job, I know I will fail, and I will be fired."

- **IRRATIONALITY:** "There is no way I can do this. Not only will I be fired, but everyone on my team will be fired as well. I'll let everyone down. We'll all be on welfare and it will be my fault. I should just quit before the presentation and save everyone the agony of my ineptitude."

- **BAD HABIT:** "There's no way I can do this. I'll ask John to do it. He's much better at these presentations than me and this way I won't put my job at risk."

Fearful thoughts involve losing something and fear this will lead to some dire prediction for the future. These thoughts have tremendous power over our ability to take action because they sound so practical and like they are ensuring our emotional and physical survival.

Irrational thoughts are tricky as well, but a little easier to catch due to the fantastic nature of the thought progression. Before long, an irrational thought will have you fully imagining your worst-case scenario. Lackluster presentation = no job = homelessness and unemployment = despair and disappointment.

Bad habit thoughts are perhaps the most difficult negative thoughts to intercept for obvious reasons. You have been thinking these thoughts for years. You've come to accept them as truth. Bad habits always interfere with positive action. A habitual negative response to stress for example, is to reach for something which might alleviate that stress and not only includes such "solutions" as alcohol and drugs, but more insidious stress relievers such as avoiding the activity entirely.

A habitual negative reaction to a situation that elicits the shy-response will always entail some type of avoidance. When you avoid, elide, sidestep, or in any way get yourself out of a social or public situation, be it personal or at work, you are avoiding and using your habitual negative thought process to reinforce your decision to not engage in an uncomfortable situation.

F.I.B.

Fear: Loss of what we have and fear of future loss

Irrationality: Dramatic life-and-death scenarios

Bad Habit: Avoidance

This all brings us back to our initial task. We can approach being fun-shy with another tool which will help us in our quest for greater comfort in social situations. Along with Thought Stopping and Acting as If, when you find yourself being hyper-vigilant and self-consciously observing yourself in the company of others, at a party for example, you can:

1. Notice the thoughts which enter your mind.

2. Name them.

3. Take a deep breath and let them go.

Once you clear the F.I.B. from your thinking, you will be in the present moment and ready for anything! You are now open to, and available to, an interesting social exchange.

There may be some people out there who are truly afraid of having a good time and enjoying themselves (let's hope they are not family members!). But by fun-shy we mean being fearful of the environment or situation required for the good time to take place. Test your irrational fears when they arise. Challenge them. Talk back to them. Gain power over them. You can choose to feel happy and hopeful in any social situation, but you must first silence the self-conscious negative voice. This is not achieved by any aggressive means. You don't want to fight fire with fire here.

This voice has been damaging enough to your feelings of self-esteem. Think of putting out the fire with a bucket of the water of truth. You can take away the mysterious power these thoughts seem to have on you by staring them down and calling them by their true names: Fear, Irrationality, and Bad Habit.

THE ART OF CONVERSATION

Much has been written on this subject. In this book, we will skip the usual tips on how to be a brilliant conversationalist, which usually includes practicing witty repartee and memorizing humorous anecdotes, preferably about the rich and famous who, preferably, you know on a first-name basis. *The Shyness Solution* will focus on some simple practical skills which you will find work like a charm in helping you to initiate and sustain a conversation with someone you would *want* to speak with.

"Want" is emphasized here because often it seems shy people will consider any social interaction a success. While this may be true on some level, hopefully by the end of this book, you will have the confidence and feelings of self-worth to choose whether a certain conversation with a certain person is something you wish to engage in or whether you would rather move on to an interaction which may be more fun and stimulating to you.

Shy people are often so grateful that anyone at all strikes up a conversation with them, that they end up either being seated next to or choosing to sit next to the overbearing bore of the party who will talk your ear off and whom everyone else is avoiding like the plague.

In the past you may have been zeroed in on by these personality types who have an uncanny ability to pick out a good listener from a crowd. You may even have felt a bit relieved to be next to one at a dinner party. But one-sided tirades do not make a conversation. And since the object here is to have some fun—which entails taking some risks— some new interpersonal skills are needed as you engage in the art of conversation.

Shy people often report not knowing what to talk about when they find themselves in a group of people, like a coffee break at the work environment for example. If you can clarify for yourself the things you are passionate about, you will be amazed at how easy it can be to converse with others. Small talk may be difficult for you. But it can be learned very easily. Talking about the weather may be an icebreaker, but you may be at a loss for where to go from there. Part of the art of conversation involves some motivation and commitment on your part.

Be Informed

You don't have to read every page of *The New York Times* Sunday edition, but if there are a few areas you have a particular interest in such as art, real estate, finance, or music, stay informed about new developments in these areas. Many of the suggestions for shy people regarding learning to converse socially offer this as a helpful tool in both initiating and sustaining a conversation.

Educate Yourself

Learn the details of three major events occurring in the

outside world. Whether it is the trial of a celebrity, a catastrophic natural disaster, or something of importance in your local community, know the details well enough that you can have an informed opinion about the matter being discussed. When we say educate, we are going to keep it simple. You don't need to read *The History of Civilization* to have an informed chat about the current political situation of your particular environment. Depending on your personal style or comfort level, this could range from reading the headline stories in *USA Today*, *People*, *The New Yorker*, or *National Geographic*. Read material you are interested in. You don't need to know the theory of quantum physics if you are standing outside and comment on the beauty of the full moon and a sky full of stars. Television news programs may also be a preference for some. These three things should include but not be limited to:

- → The main news story of the moment.

- → The arts. What is the current or upcoming exhibition at your local museum or theater? Talking about this may even lead to an invitation to view it together.

- → Something from popular culture. Gossip about which movie star is having an affair with which senator isn't absolutely necessary, but may not hurt either.

These three topics can be a springboard for deeper conversations. You will probably be very surprised at how easy it is for you to talk about these subjects since they are usually well known to all.

Find Your Passion

What are you passionate about? Art, antiques, your work, movies, plays, books, current events, politics, social policy, sports, religion, cooking? Identify one area where you could never run out of things to talk about (we all have at least one) and use this as your "fall-back" topic if the conversation seems to lag or run out of steam. If you are a sports fan, and you know others in the room are also interested in sports, even a cliché question like "How about them Yankees?" will not only show you have a sense of humor, but will keep the other person or people on their toes since you will be ready to have a healthy debate if you are armed with the confidence of your feelings of passion about the subject.

If you are an avid fan of foreign films, you might mention one you'd recently seen and comment on its merits or lack of good ones recently. Others will chime in with their thoughts on movies and you may find yourself in a lively discussion with all sides participating.

Believe it or not, you will not feel shy with others as long as the subject you are discussing is one about which you are informed, educated, and passionate.

BE A PRIVATE EYE

Another tool for easing into the art of conversation is imagining yourself as a researcher, private investigator, or laboratory assistant. Your "job" is to ask questions and uncover information. Everyone and especially non-shy people love to be asked questions about themselves. Ask about what they do, about their families, about their interests, etc. This communication skill is something a shy person is usually not practiced in. It's difficult for the shy to imagine anyone actually *wanting* to be asked questions about themselves since prior to being shy-strong, you may have dreaded these types of interactions.

Remember, this is not an interrogation process. You are simply imagining yourself in a role. Remind yourself to use your tool of Acting as If. In utilizing this tool you will be able to distance yourself from your self-consciousness. Tell yourself you have a job to do. You are researching a friend's life. How has it been since you last saw her? What has she been doing? What has changed? Be interested, curious, and inquisitive.

If you are on a date, and you use this technique, you may want to imagine you are interviewing the other person to learn about who he or she is, what he or she is interested in, what makes him or her feel alive and what doesn't.

This exercise isn't about clinical detachment or any sort of scientific exploration. It's an exploration involving engaged curiosity. And it can be quite fun if you approach it lightheartedly and with a sense of humor about yourself and your "role" and the method you are using to learn about another person. You are choosing a nontraditional approach here because it creates the space you need in order not to feel overwhelmed by the intimacy of talking one to one, which you need to practice, practice, practice with gusto! The "Being a Researcher" technique is a great way to get this practice so you will have more enjoyment in your social interactions.

BODY LANGUAGE

One of the most important components in the art of conversing has nothing to do with talking. Our body language can sometimes say more than you even want it to! The following are some typical body language habits of the shy person. If you recognize any of these as something you do, you may want to consider changing these habits because they may send a message you don't wish to convey.

Eye Contact

Shy people have difficulty making and sustaining eye contact. You may be afraid you will blush uncontrollably or feel very uncomfortable if you maintain eye contact for any length of time, but this is perhaps the single most important aspect of good communication skills.

Lack of eye contact has been cited as the predominant feature involved in mistrust and leads to the belief that a person is devious or deceptive. You must remember that the non-shy do not immediately assume another person is shy if the person cannot maintain eye contact. Most people assume at best this lowering of the gaze is due to disinterest, and at worst, rudeness and unreliability. So go ahead, dare to look someone you are speaking to in the eyes. If it feels too intense at first and you must look away, return your contact as soon as possible. Even if you are only able to tolerate this for a few seconds, keep returning your gaze after a few moments. This will become easier as you practice. The most important thing to remember is to keep to your comfort level and keep trying. Sporadic eye contact is much better than none at all and will keep the other person from mis-interpreting your timidity for disinterest or boredom.

Posture

An interesting study would be the correlation between self-consciousness and shy behaviors and body posture. Many people who sit huddled with slumped shoulders, or shoulders raised around their ears, who do not walk with shoulders back and head erect, often describe themselves as shy.

Simply changing your posture can effect a major change in your attitude and how you feel about yourself. When you are holding your body in a confident way, you will project a different personality than if you are curled in the fetal position on the couch. Imagine a person slumped over a table in a restaurant, huddled in the corner at a party, and now imagine that same person (yourself, perhaps?), walking into the restaurant or standing at a party with your head held high, and with a natural straight back and a look of interest on your face as you scan the room. These two differing scenarios are obvious as to the different messages they convey about you and how you feel about yourself.

The exercises in this chapter, done with practice and again, keeping them fun and challenging and tailored to your comfort level, will assist you in "getting out of your own way" as our friend Karen put it so well, and will thereby enable you to add fun and enjoyment to any social situation you choose to engage in.

CHAPTER SIX: "If we deny love that is given to us, if we refuse to give love because we fear pain or loss, then our lives will be empty, our loss greater. If you fear nothing, you love nothing. If you love nothing, what joy can there be in life?"

—Unknown

This chapter is for those of you who long to have romance, but find it difficult to manifest and sustain loving relationships. For the shy person, dating can be extremely stressful. Part of the human condition is to experience conflict and ambivalence when confronted with the issue of solitude vs. intimacy. For the timid, solitude is not as uncomfortable an experience as it is for the non-shy. Just as being alone can be excruciating for most extroverts, intimacy with another can elicit the same uncomfortable feelings in the introvert.

Why is intimacy so difficult? Because it requires risk. The risk of exposing our vulnerabilities, which many shy people avoid like the mall at Christmastime. Having spent years protecting yourself and attempting to hide your shyness, the prospect of letting go of this comfortable shell and allowing another into your life can be a bit frightening. But the good news is, by using your tools of Thought Stopping, transforming negative thoughts into positive ones, Acting as If, and redefining your belief that shyness is a liability into shyness is a strength, you can and will have a successful and loving relationship.

You must start slowly, however. It took years for you to develop a persona where intimacy is not easy, so being able to be close with someone will not happen overnight! Intimate closeness is built upon trust. This is another thing which may not come easily to the shy. Trust is built upon experience. Experiencing yourself and your love interest in a variety of situations, both fun and easy and also difficult will build the trust you need to risk getting closer to someone else. The key ingredient for the intimacy-shy to allow yourself to get close to another and to allow the other to get close to you, lies in exposure.

As you spend more and more time together, you will begin to feel more comfortable with yourself in your partner's presence. Comfort with yourself is the first step in allowing someone to move closer toward you. You will need to experience and expose yourself to a variety of intimate situations, such as a quiet dinner at a romantic, candlelit restaurant, a walk in a park, or at the movies or theater.

As you literally expose yourself (your vulnerability anyway!) to these different experiences you will develop more confidence in your ability to handle situations you may have been previously fearful to engage in.

Many people wonder if they should divulge the fact that they have experienced painful shyness in their lives to a new love interest. The answer is a resounding yes! Getting to know someone, and letting them get to know you, can be fun, exciting, and sometimes a little scary. It is important that you let your partner know that while you may be quiet at times, it is not anything they should take personally. You can let them know that solving your shyness and becoming stronger is a challenge which you are happily engaged in dealing with.

Everyone can be insecure to some degree and in certain situations. You don't want someone you are interested in to interpret your quiet demeanor as aloof disinterest. Even though you will employ your strategies of Acting as If and Thought Stopping on dates as well, you will probably want to let your partner know you sometimes feel uncomfortable with conversation in a group for example, so that he or she does not feel they are boring or uninteresting to you! The following techniques will come in handy in love-shy situations.

NAME THAT FEELING

In dating as in other social areas, it is helpful to either say out loud, or to yourself, what you are feeling. We will go into this at length in the last chapter, "Putting It All Together," but for now, Naming a Feeling will serve a couple of purposes which will be useful to you in your dating life.

David describes how naming his feelings worked for him:

"I was seeing this great girl for about two months and I still hadn't gotten the nerve to kiss her. We'd been on six dates. The first one was horrible and I thought she would never go out with me again. I don't drink much and I ended up having three glasses of wine because I was so nervous but it just made me feel stupid and I ended up getting more self-conscious and of course feeling wrecked the next day didn't help .

I finally got the courage to call her a few days later to see if she wanted to go out again, figuring either she'd say no or not pick up the phone, but she actually sounded happy to hear from me! So the next date I didn't have to get trashed to talk to her and we had a great time. By date number four I really wanted to kiss her goodnight, but I was way too nervous. The next date I spent the entire time worrying about the last five minutes to come at the end and whether I'd be able to kiss her. I wasn't.

Now it's date six and I just decided when she asked me at one point if I was okay. I must have looked panic-stricken or something, because I wasn't in the present at all, just thinking about when the time came to say goodnight. I decided to tell her the truth. I told her I liked her and really wanted to kiss her goodnight, but I was nervous and wasn't sure if I should and before I could get the rest of the sentence out she reached over and kissed me!"

No promises here that naming your feelings out loud will elicit as dramatic a response as David received, but the basic premise remains. When we state how we feel in any given moment, "I feel nervous right now," this will lead to a "why" response: "Because I want to go on a date with this person who is interested in me." And then you can name the thought causing the feeling which usually contains some element of fear or insecurity.

It's a circular process. Thought creates a "why" response which creates a feeling which creates fear which leads to avoidance:

Thought: I'm afraid to ask her out.

Why: Because she'll probably say no.

Feeling: I am such a loser.

Fear/Avoidance: I won't ask her. This way I won't get hurt.

Once you recognize this cycle of self-defeating insecurity-based thinking you can deploy your arsenal of Thought Stopping and negative thought replacement:

Thought: I'm afraid to ask her out.

Why: Because she might say no.

Feeling: I am a loser.

STOP THOUGHT: "No, I am fun to be with and I have a lot to offer someone in a relationship. I'll take a risk and ask her out. Nothing ventured, nothing gained."

BE YOURSELF

All of the exercises we've learned so far are designed to help you feel comfortable with just simply being who you are. And coming to the realization that you don't need to be more than that. You've learned how many wonderful traits you possess by virtue of your sensitive nature. Now it's time to allow yourself to be, fully, who you truly are. Someone who is interested in you is interested in all facets of you. If that person is not, then move on and quickly. You will only deepen and encourage more interest on his or her part if you risk being honest and being yourself.

Hiding our true nature is not attractive, whether it's our external beauty and accomplishments or internal accomplishments derived from looking hard at ourselves and having the courage to change. Dare to take the chance to let someone get to know you and you will be delighted to find it becomes easier to get close to others and allow them to see the real you.

Shame is the unspoken secret of the painfully shy. By now you understand that your shyness, being a part of you and not all of you, is nothing to be ashamed of. To the contrary, you may find your modest, quiet personality is extremely seductive to members of the opposite sex.

As we've learned, talking to others in a social situation is not easy for the habitually shy. Becoming friends with others requires risks that are difficult, and expanding this risk-taking to include intimate relationships involving love. Partnership and marriage is territory you may have felt was off limits to you. You may even have felt that your shyness would prohibit you from engaging in a healthy relationship

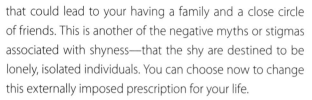

that could lead to your having a family and a close circle of friends. This is another of the negative myths or stigmas associated with shyness—that the shy are destined to be lonely, isolated individuals. You can choose now to change this externally imposed prescription for your life.

You can choose to have intimacy and closeness with another human being. You will not be exempt from all the difficult issues that arise in love relationships for everyone, but you will not be alone and you will enjoy a rich, full life.

Tips For Successful Dating

→ Go slowly.

→ Be yourself.

→ Name your feelings when appropriate.

→ Risk being vulnerable.

→ Don't be afraid to have a good time!

DATE, DATE, DATE

For the lucky few of you out there, you may meet your soul mate on your first date. Stranger things have happened! But for the rest of you, do go on every date you are asked out on. Refuse no offers. This may be pushing you out of your comfort zone, but what you are actually doing by dating frequently is practicing. And if you have been shy in your love life, you need lots of practice!

Even if you find someone is "not your type," go out to lunch or dinner anyway. You'll experience yourself in different settings with different types of people and curiously enough, this will help you learn not only how to converse with another person, but you will learn much about yourself. How else are you going to recognize your soul mate when she or he walks into your life, unless you have had lots and lots of less than starry-eyed dating encounters? And some of these people may even become friends.

OK, you say. This all sounds great. But how do you meet people? The following is a list of possible places and ways to comfortably engage with others and possibly meet that special someone.

WORK IT OUT

The gym is a great place to meet new people. And it can't hurt to also feel confident about your physical appearance when you're contemplating dating! Remember to use your shy-strength and dare to make eye contact and smile. If you keep your eyes glued to the floor as you move through the weight-lifting machines, you may miss an opportunity for conversation with a member of the opposite sex.

If you don't already belong to one, visit several gymnasiums. If you want to meet a guy, you obviously don't want to join a women's-only gym. If you're a guy looking for a female love interest, stay away from the more macho, weight-lifting focused gyms, which cater to the testosterone crowd.

Shop around. Most gyms will give you a tour or a day pass and you can use this opportunity to check out the vibe of the place and whether or not you feel comfortable there. Try to go to the gym either early in the morning or after work, when most people attend. Lunch break is also a good time, but people tend to be more in a hurry and less inclined to engage in small talk.

Choose classes that are coed, such as spinning or kickboxing. A guy looking to meet a woman might venture into the predominantly female high-impact aerobics class and as he will be greatly outnumbered, the women will probably be more than curious about his presence. Women will find opportunities to speak with men if they venture into the free-weight section. Men are often more than happy to give advice on correct weight-lifting techniques to the few women who are brave enough to walk into their territory.

One of the best areas in the gym to strike up a conversation, or have someone talk to you, is in the treadmill section. Try using the elliptical machines since they are more conducive to chatting than the treadmill on which people tend to be very serious about getting in their ten miles in forty-five minutes. Many gyms now even have individual television sets that are listened to via headphones. Whatever you do, don't wear headphones or read a book or magazine. Try to stay away from these distractions from interaction.

When you walk into the gym, scan the room. Perhaps you'll notice someone who interests you and you may decide to ride the stationary bike or machine next to him or her. Smile and say hello if possible. If the person is single and is also looking to meet someone, be open to any conversation that might ensue. If one-on-one exchanges are too much for you to handle at this point in your quest to solve your shyness, you might try some of the other group activities offered, such as beginning (or advanced) tennis, racquetball, hiking, or running. Most gyms have a bulletin board prominently displayed with sign-up sheets for group endeavors. If you do find you fancy someone, make sure you go back to the gym at the same time of day if possible. Many people have a set routine and time for exercising. And it may feel more comfortable to talk to someone after you have both noticed and had a few nonverbal (eye-contact) exchanges at the water fountain with each other.

BOOKSTORES

Bookstores have become one of the best ways to meet new people. Many even have cafés where you can sit down and whatever you do, not read a book! After putting on your best Researcher/Acting as If persona, walk over to your favorite section. Is it Philosophy? Fiction? Bestsellers? Fly-fishing?

A well-known secret is that the travel section is a good place to strike up a conversation with someone. If you've always wanted to go to Tibet, pick up a book and browse through it. If you notice someone interesting looking at a book on Italy and you've been there you might even ask if he or she is traveling there for the first time? If the answer is yes, you'll have something to talk about. Of course, you know the best, not-to-be-missed restaurant in Rome, tucked away down a labyrinthine street. If the person has been there before, you might compare notes.

What this all amounts to is this: Certain topics, such as travel, are less intimidating to talk about with someone you don't know and have never met before. Everyone has something to say about the places traveled to and adventures had. If you or they have been to a certain country before, you can compare notes. If you are in the self-help section and looking at books on oh, say, shyness for example, you may just find yourself engaging in conversation with someone else interested in the same topic, and there will be no problem for either of you in discussing this subject!

Many bookstores offer talks with authors and other topics of interest. This particular venue has become a very popular way to meet others. At the very least, you'll have an interesting evening and learn something you can bring up at your next party or other social gathering. Go to as many of these discussions as your schedule permits, but make a special effort to attend talks on subjects you are most interested in, since these are situations where you are most likely to meet someone who shares a common interest.

Try to sample many different bookstore environments, from the larger chain stores to the smaller specialty ones. If you have an avid interest in photography, for example, find a store that specializes in this area. Ask to be put on their mailing list so you can stay informed of any upcoming events you might like to attend.

DEVELOP A SPIRITUAL PRACTICE

If you already belong to a traditional denominational church, chances are you are aware of several opportunities to meet people with whom you share a belief system. Many churches also have affiliations with organizations for single or divorced members to meet others of like mind. You may wish to speak to your pastor or priest to learn more about this. If your particular church is not an option for meeting new people, you may wish to attend churches in other areas of your community.

If you have a personal spiritual practice such as meditation, yoga, or a general interest in holistic healing or Eastern philosophy, joining a group or attending seminars is a wonderful way to meet others who share similar thinking. Developing a spiritual practice can greatly enhance all areas of your life and will enrich any potential partnership.

BECOME A VOLUNTEER

Volunteering your time to a worthy cause is not only good for the world and for yourself, but it is a terrific way to meet other single people who have an interested in belonging to a group devoted to doing selfless work to help others less fortunate. Choose a cause you are interested in, whether it's helping disadvantaged children, animal rights, or volunteering in a hospital; you will be surrounded by wonderful people such as yourself who wish to make the world a kinder place. You can locate these organizations through your church, the community service listing in your telephone book, or via the Internet.

TALK TO YOUR FRIENDS

Sometimes the most obvious solutions are the most difficult to see. Let your friends and acquaintances know that you are ready to take the gigantic step of including another person in your life.

You know this won't be easy, but you are now up for the challenge. You can face your fear with a "choice" statement, such as "I choose to meet someone who I can have a meaningful relationship with because I want to feel less lonely and isolated."

Perhaps your friends have been constantly trying to set you up with someone or other on a date, but until now, you have been reluctant to take them up on their offers. They may have even given up trying. So, talk to them. Ask them if they know any single people who they think might be appropriate for you to date. Remember, this isn't marriage! It is simply dating and you will need to meet lots of potential suitors before you find "the one," unless you are very lucky and meet someone very special early on in your dating experiences.

Your friends will more than likely be happy to oblige your request. Often, in just making the request you will see the "A-ha!" response which will tell you they know just the person and they can't believe they hadn't thought of him or her before. Dating someone your friends have set you up with also has the added benefit of being able to spend time on a date with mutual acquaintances, which can add to your comfort level in the beginning, when finding things to talk about may be challenging.

SIGN UP FOR WORKSHOPS AND CLASSES

Have you always wanted to learn falconry? Pottery? Gardening? Guitar? Astrology? Taking a class either at an arts center or a continuing education institution is a fabulous way to meet people. And you will be learning something new at the same time! Check out the bulletin board at your local post office, the health food store, or museum/gallery. Local haunts such as coffee shops, smaller, bohemian-type restaurants, and art supply stores often have a networking site where fliers and other notices for classes and opportunities are posted.

JOIN A GROUP

Along these same lines, there are many wonderful groups to join where you might meet people who share similar interests. Do you like to mountain bike, horseback ride, or take long walks in nature? Attend the theater or opera? There are groups for everything. Feel free to be creative in your search. If bicycling is something you love to do, go to your local cycle shop and inquire about any group outings. If they don't have the information, ask for some suggestions as to who might. And if you are feeling exceptionally shy-strong, put up your own notice saying you are looking for people to ride with on weekends.

If you love art, music, or plays, contact your favorite museum or gallery and ask about group tours. You can also get in touch with your local community center or chamber of commerce. The Internet may also be of help in finding groups you might like to join.

THE INTERNET

The reason this option for meeting others is last on the list is simple. Staying home alone in front of your computer is not the optimal way to finally solve your issues of shyness. Many people who are too shy to date have described spending weeks, months, even years(!) chatting or IMing people on dating sites and never getting up the nerve to meet with them in person.

The previous suggestions for meeting people require you to be proactive in your search to find a partner. Actively making a commitment to challenge your habitual shyness and getting out there in the world is what will bring you closer toward your goal of greater self-confidence.

Internet dating sites may fit your comfort level like the proverbial glove, but you will not be challenging yourself to confront and overcome your fears unless you take an active role and personal responsibility for meeting others.

The Internet *can* be a great resource for meeting someone. But if you do choose this route, make sure you actually *meet* with them. Again, as in any dating, meet any and all people you feel you might have a rapport or something in common with. Even if they don't turn out to be the love of your life, you will gain experience in talking to another person one to one and you may even make some friends in the process.

Remember to use your discretion. Being shy carries with it both excellent observational skills and on the other hand, a willingness to forgo your intuition and enter into social interactions which might not be what you truly want, but are doing so because you are grateful and relieved someone, anyone, would want to meet you. This tendency will be explored in depth in the next chapter, but for now, suffice to say, you should neither wait a month to meet with someone you are interested in, nor should you agree to meet after one online exchange.

In meeting for the first time, *you* should pick the time and place. The time for a first meeting should preferably be in the afternoon or early evening. Choose a place you are comfortable in, perhaps one you frequent. This probably goes without saying, but if at any point you start to experience an uneasy feeling due to inappropriate talk or behavior from the other person, you are perfectly justified to excuse yourself and leave. Meeting and getting to know someone does not include tolerating bad behavior.

Research Internet dating sites. There are hundreds of them out there, but only a handful are reputed to be reliable and a productive use of your time. Some even screen for potential "crackpots," ensuring you will not be exposed to an unpleasant experience, which is extremely important as you make your first venture out into the world of dating.

No names or preferences for Internet dating services will be given here, but a list of resources where you can find links to matchmaking sites is included in this book starting on page 137. There is also the possibility that you have a friend, acquaintance, coworker, or family member who may guide you to the best site for you. Keep in mind, if you are looking for a long-term relationship for example, you don't want to waste your time on sites which advertise themselves as "Singles looking for a fling." The same

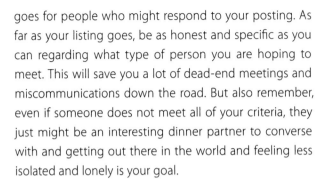

goes for people who might respond to your posting. As far as your listing goes, be as honest and specific as you can regarding what type of person you are hoping to meet. This will save you a lot of dead-end meetings and miscommunications down the road. But also remember, even if someone does not meet all of your criteria, they just might be an interesting dinner partner to converse with and getting out there in the world and feeling less isolated and lonely is your goal.

CHAPTER SEVEN: " If you explore beneath shyness or party chitchat, you can sometimes turn a dull exchange into an intriguing one. I've found this to be particularly true in the case of professors or intellectuals, who are full of fascinating information, but need encouragement before they'll divulge it. "

—*Joyce Carol Oates*

" The way you overcome shyness is to become so wrapped up in something that you forget to be afraid. "

—*Lady Bird Johnson*

If you have ever heard someone described as "the life of the party," it probably conjures up the image of a person who is talkative, friendly, funny, and at times outrageous in their social behavior. This is the type of person who would never be described as "shy," "introverted," or "timid."

The truth is that while the extrovert may elicit a lot of attention, anyone who has attended or hosted a party knows that any interesting gathering is comprised of many different types of people. And while someone may be the first person to jump up and dance on the bar, the majority in attendance will be amused onlookers at the spectacle.

For our purposes, "life" will be another word for heart and soul. And the heart of any party is in the shared experience had by all invited. People who describe themselves as shy often feel if they are not the extrovert holding court over an enraptured crowd, then their presence is not valued. Shy people may even feel a bit envious of their flamboyant fellow partygoer and wish they could be as uninhibited in the company of others.

The shy-strong have come to understand that although they may enjoy the antics of the extrovert, they do not need to match their energy or style in order to both have a good time and feel that they too have a valuable place in the room.

"All or nothing" expectations of ourselves in social situations—"Either I am outgoing and fascinating company or I am boring and have no right to be here"—are examples of the self-defeating thinking that must be turned upside down and replaced with a new belief system.

Yes, even those who consider themselves shy can be the life or heart and soul of any party or social gathering. Understand that your shy-strength is every bit as compelling as the person who is the first to drag out the karaoke machine.

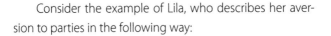

Consider the example of Lila, who describes her aversion to parties in the following way:

"I've always dreaded any kind of party, no matter if it was just a few people or a New Year's Eve party with 100. This was especially the case when I was in college. My roommate was very popular and she was always trying to get me to come with her to parties. Half the time I would make excuses why I couldn't go and half the time I'd force myself, but I never had a good time. No one ever talked to me and I was too shy to talk to anyone anyway. It got to be so painful to just sit there, miserable and counting the minutes until I could leave, that I just stopped going out completely.

After a couple of months I realized I had absolutely no social life. My roommate had even stopped asking me to go anywhere with her. I was talking to her one night, feeling sorry for myself that I didn't have any friends and she told me it was my own fault. I told her 'No, it was because I was shy,' and she said, 'No, it's because you don't make any effort. Lots of people like you very much, but you just can't see it.' I couldn't believe what I was hearing.

Then she gave me some advice I'll never forget: She said lots of people at parties feel shy and awkward and if I would just try to talk to some of them I would have a good time. I was reluctant, but we made a plan and I went with her to a dorm party that weekend. I still had the same anxious feeling and wanted to run out of the room, but I didn't. That night, she was really a terrific friend. She kept making eye contact with me and pointing out people I should go sit next to and I thought, What the heck, if this doesn't work out, I'll never have to go through another one of these things again.

There was this really cute guy sitting on the couch by himself going through the CD collection and I went over and sat next to him and forced myself to say something about the music being boring, which it was, and he looked at me for what seemed like forever and then he smiled and said he was thinking the same thing. And then he asked me if I wanted to help him find something better. So we sat there, going through this pile of CDs, talking about what kind of music we liked and didn't like, which led into a conversation about a ton of other things, and when it was time to go, I didn't want to leave!

I made a new friend that night and I learned a big lesson about how sometimes having a good time requires some effort on my part. I can't say I jump at the chance to go to parties, but when I do, I always try to find one thing I can do or say to someone who looks like they're feeling like I do. So far, it's worked every time and I've made some wonderful new friends."

As you can see, Lila took a risk. Any successful relationship requires risking your vulnerability and pushing your comfort level a bit so that you can open yourself up to the possibility of making a connection with another person.

Parties and social gatherings can be anxiety producing for many people, and not only for those who consider themselves shy. Following are some things you can do however, to minimize the fearful aspect of these group situations.

BRING ALONG A FRIEND

Any accompaniment by a good friend will be helpful, but preferably you should ask a friend who is not struggling with issues of shyness to come along with you. Having someone you feel comfortable with at your side is obviously less anxiety-provoking than entering into a room full of strangers. Strategize with your friend before the party. Let the friend know you want to try something different. You want to experiment with being fearless or at least being less fearful. Ask your friend to help you with this. If he or she is more outgoing, he or she might go up and speak to people and then summon you to join in, or may be savvy enough to know how to bring the conversation around to a topic you feel comfortable talking about. Perhaps you might even take the bold step of having a signal for your friend, where he or she can move off tactfully if you are engaging in a conversation easily.

HANG AROUND THE FOOD

The food is always where the action is at any party. Depending on the setting, this may be a banquet table or the kitchen. Everyone eventually makes their way to this area and if you are close by, the chances are very good that someone who is alone will say hello. Remember to make your eye contact and smile, keeping your posture and body language open for dialogue. If you are standing in a corner staring at your plate, people who might have wished to speak to you will walk by, sensing you do not want to be disturbed.

TALK TO ANYONE

People who enjoy themselves at social gatherings talk to anyone and everyone they can. Not all at once of course! A friend described a woman she observed at a party having a fabulous time. The woman was in her sixties and this was the thirtieth birthday party for a coworker. She didn't keep to herself due to the age difference, but chatted away with the younger people, asking them what they did and seemed genuinely interested in hearing what they had to say. Even if she couldn't contribute to the pop culture topics, she asked questions and made references and inferences from her own generation and experience and was completely embraced and accepted by the younger crowd.

So, don't let age, cultural background, sex, or style of dress allow you to make a judgment that you will have nothing in common. This is one of the secrets of being the life or heart of the party. Be open to any conversation with anyone, regardless of what you perceive may be differences. You may be surprised to learn you have much in common.

KEEP YOUR EYES OPEN

Being shy-strong, you have developed a keen intuitive awareness and ability to observe others. This ability was honed from years of standing on the sidelines, watching others interact, but without you participating. You can now choose to use this gift in service of your goal to become part of any social dynamic.

At a social gathering for instance, watch the group. If it's helpful to you, remember to use your investigator or researcher persona. Study the gathering. Are there certain people you might like to meet? Is anyone standing off alone? Do you see someone who seems approachable? Watch for eye contact from others and muster your resolve to meet their gaze, if only for a couple of seconds.

As you well know, feeling timid can actually make you reluctant to scan a room with confidence and interest. If you do choose to sit on a comfortable couch away from the action, by all means don't pick up a book from the coffee table and bury your face in it! Stay alert and watchful, glancing around the room and before long your eyes will be met by someone else's and you may find yourself engaged in conversation before long, perhaps even about the book you didn't choose to hide in.

GAUGE YOUR COMFORT LEVEL

At a party or larger social gathering, it is important that you check in with yourself often to see how comfortable you are feeling. Let's take a scale from 1 to 10, 10 being extremely comfortable and 1 being feeling like you want to race out the door. Measure where you are at as you try to go up one level.

You walk into the room and feel at level 1. You decide to push this to a 2. So you take off your coat and sit down. Get comfortable at this level and then move on to 3. You walk over and get yourself a drink and something to eat. Stay here at this level for a while as you replace your negative thoughts with positive ones and do your deep breathing. You are now at 4. You glance around the room for someone who you intuit you will feel comfortable talking to. Make eye contact. Stay with this level for a few minutes. If the person does not approach you, but seems interested in talking, move on to level 5 and walk over in his or her direction.

Remember all this is done incrementally and in stages. You are acclimating yourself to the environment much the same way a mountain climber does when adjusting to high altitudes.

Don't expect to rush into a party, grab a drink, and start chatting with the first person you see. If you ease yourself into situations which have been difficult in the past, you will find each step, if taken slowly, is not as hard as it seems. When you think too much about it in terms of the entire process, without breaking it into steps, a situation like this can be overwhelming. Remember, you are climbing a staircase and taking one step at a time. You can tell yourself that you can stop at any point. But the goal is to both manage your fear and push yourself a little further once you feel the fear has dissipated a bit.

In managing your comfort level it is very important that you don't push yourself too far. If you get to a comfort level of 8 or so and want to really challenge your fear by joining in a game of charades, by all means, do! But you may be just as content to be an active observer, enjoying the game from a comfortable perch, at a safe distance. You are your own guide here. Use your intuition. You will know when you are reacting from a fearful place and not pushing yourself a bit further when you are indeed perfectly able to do so. You will also know when you are truly not ready to take a step further out of your comfort zone, just as you will know when you are ready for this.

As with all of the exercises in this book, try not to pass judgment on yourself. After all, you made it to the party and you are making a valiant effort to further enhance your shy-strength by attempting to interact and connect with others. And that desire is the true life of any party.

CHAPTER EIGHT: "A true friend knows your weaknesses but shows you your strengths; feels your fears but fortifies your faith; sees your anxieties but frees your spirit; recognizes your disabilities but emphasizes your possibilities."

—*William Arthur Ward*

Maintaining your sense of self and your commitment to transforming your shyness into strength can be a daunting task indeed, when in the company of other people who are extremely extroverted. When surrounded by the non-shy, people with a more quiet and reserved demeanor, which can often be described as "shyness," tend to withdraw even further from a conversation or social interaction.

This challenge presents a great opportunity for you to practice your shy-strong exercises and can give you an even deeper commitment to redefining your previous negative assumptions about what it means to be shy.

We have discussed how gentleness and tact are a couple of the attributes you inherently possess. Since the old adage that opposites attract is observed time and again, you may find if you take a look at your life and the significant people in it, there are a great many extroverts you are in association with. You may also find that many people in your life are rather "difficult" personality types. There is no coincidence here. By definition, your quiet nature allows you to be able to tolerate a lot of behaviors that a more assertive personality would not be able to handle.

If the loud and commanding—and there is no judgment here as to this being a negative personality trait, it is simply a certain expression of a personal style—happens to be someone you have frequent interaction with, like a boss or coworker, you may have made yourself more quiet and less visible in order to balance the energy level of your social exchange. If this is the case, you must be aware of the toll this relationship takes on you in terms of stress and the need you feel to repress your own feelings.

Shy people are great peacemakers. You are also often eager to please and this can put you in the position of having to listen to and absorb a lot of emotional expression from others which can include anger. The other person may even believe that you are very strong, since most people would challenge, question, or otherwise talk back to them.

They admire your ability to be a tree in the hurricane of their demonstrative style and may come to depend on you for this ability you have that others do not.

What they don't know, is that this is not strength at all unless you understand and accept that you are *choosing* to use your reserve and tact in dealing with a difficult person who you must deal with on a daily basis, especially in the case of an employer or manager.

There are ways for you to withstand a difficult personality type without stuffing your true feelings and filling yourself with worry and stress.

If the loud person in your life whom you find yourself being extra quiet around is a spouse or family member, the same holds true as for other relationships, although there is a slight difference. Say your husband, wife, or significant other is a dyed-in-the-wool extrovert, who has come to rely on and expect you to be submissive and nonconfrontational with regards to your interactions with him or her. As you begin to try to change this dynamic you may be met with at best, surprise, and at worst, resistance.

We'll discuss assertiveness later, but for now, the most important thing for you to grasp is that your "shyness" is a *reaction* to your exposure to overt extroversion and not the cause.

Think about whom you feel most comfortable around. Are these people quiet and gentle or outgoing and boisterous? You may recall the example of Jim, whose large extended family were either "hollerers" or "screechers." His reaction to all this clamoring for attention was to withdraw into his room and listen to soothing music. As you've learned, your shyness has given you many admirable qualities. One of these characteristics may also be sensitivity to certain personality types.

If you find yourself feeling uncomfortable around very loud and demonstrative people, this doesn't mean there is anything wrong with you. You are just by nature, more comfortable with people who are less aggressive in their emotional expression. Having said this, some shy people report feeling *more* comfortable around extroverts because they know there will be less demand upon them to participate. This may even have been you, before you decided to turn your shyness into strength.

The goal here is not to rid yourself of people who are extroverted and unlike you. The goal is to acquire another shy-strength—being able to be present for yourself, stick up for yourself, and hold your own while in the company of others who would never describe themselves as "shy."

If you have a loved one, family member, spouse, friend, coworker, or employer who is of the extrovert variety, you are well aware of your tendency to stay in the background, back away from any confrontation and essentially let them run the show. While this may seem like peacekeeping or just plain easier and less stressful than speaking up for what you want, it is a difficult scenario which may lead to you harboring resentments for being unheard, unappreciated, not respected and listened to and often ignored.

So! Here lies one of the biggest challenges to solving your shyness and becoming more confident. You need to become more assertive. And as any person who has experienced shyness can tell you, becoming more assertive is a scary task. But certainly not as daunting (or exhausting!) as trying to dodge and placate an aggressive personality.

ASSERTIVENESS OR AGGRESSION?

Assertiveness is defined as: "The ability to assert, to state or express positively, to affirm. To defend or maintain one's rights for example. To put oneself forward boldly in an effort to make an opinion known."

Aggression is defined as: "The act of initiating hostilities or invasion. The practice or habit of launching attacks. In psychological terms, aggression is hostile or destructive behavior or actions."

Simply stated, assertiveness is a positive action and aggression is a destructive one.

Many people confuse assertiveness with aggression. They feel if they defend or maintain their rights, they are being aggressive and hostile. The root of this confusion is difficulty with understanding the expression of anger.

This difficulty is not only in expressing one's own anger, but in the uncomfortable feelings which arise when you feel others are angry, usually not only if you believe they are angry with you, but for any reason whatsoever. We may even feel that another person is angry when they are being assertive, for example, putting themselves forward boldly or forcefully in an effort to be heard.

The terms "bold" and "forceful" are not words generally used to describe the shy. In fact, timid and submissive are the more frequent adjectives you may have become accustomed to hearing.

Why is anger so difficult for shy people? It may be in the way it is most typically expressed—loudly and with great emotion. You may even have personal reasons for labeling anger a "bad" or negative feeling. Maybe you had an angry parent, sibling, or partner. Whatever the reason, you may have come to feel that you cannot or do not have a right to express any of your own anger in any situation.

Anger is a feeling we all experience. There is nothing inherently wrong with feeling angry. Anger only becomes a "problem" when it is used to hurt, belittle, abuse, or intimidate another. There is such a thing as healthy anger. When you have been treated abusively or unfairly, you will undoubtedly feel anger. Many shy people are as afraid of their own feelings of anger as they are of others being angry with them.

When you're angry at someone, do you tell the person how you feel or do you hold the uncomfortable feeling in, fearful of repercussions, that might result from your expressing your emotions? Are you afraid the other person will get angry with you? That you might be judged harshly? That the person will no longer be your friend or might leave you or stop loving you?

The fear of disappointing another or of losing their love are the two main motivators for holding back when we feel angry. The danger in repressing our genuine feelings and especially angry ones, is that this can often contribute to our feeling powerless, hopeless, and sometimes, depressed.

Remember, being assertive does not mean being angry—although the circumstances that prompt your need to be assertive may initially cause you to feel a great deal of anger.

Assertiveness is a healthy, positive expression of your need to stand up for yourself. Many shy people would have a lot less difficulty defending someone else who is being treated badly, for example, or protesting cruelty to an animal, than they would have defending themselves.

Asserting yourself does not mean you must feel or express yourself in an angry manner. To the contrary, being assertive is confidence building and is a great tool in helping you solve your shyness. You will need to practice this many times however, before you feel comfortable with being assertive.

If you maintain that assertiveness is a positive behavior and aggression is a destructive one, you will have a guideline as to how to express yourself appropriately when you wish to have your needs met and reach your goals. You will also have a good barometer for when to be assertive: If the action taken (assertiveness) is done in order to make a positive change like standing up for your rights, allowing yourself and your feelings to be heard and noticed, protecting yourself from harm or in an attempt to further your goals, then you are being assertive. If the action taken will cause negativity and hurt, then one is engaged in being aggressive.

Let's revisit the example from the questionnaire wherein you expected a promised raise at your workplace and never received it, although coworkers have received theirs. The obvious aggressive response would be to storm into your boss's office, spewing profanities and demand your raise while threatening to quit if it is not forthcoming.

The assertive response would be to sit down with your boss and ask why you did not receive your raise. If the answer seems unfair to you (which it undoubtedly will!), you would now state your feelings on this inequality clearly and in a calm manner. You might also want to point out that others did receive their salary increase and you expect to be treated with the same respect as your coworkers.

The difference between assertiveness and aggression is anger—destructive anger. The problem most shy people face is being able to distinguish assertion from hurtful anger. Those who describe themselves as shy often feel if they stand up for their rights, they will come across to another person as confrontational and angry. This misconception is the reason many shy people do not dare to take action to achieve their goals.

The shy-strong know that asserting oneself is a win-win situation. The person attempting to take advantage of you will be put on notice that you are not to be treated unfairly, and in the meantime; you will also get what you want. The reality is, that assertiveness expressed in a non-confrontational manner is highly respected by all and the shy-strong know that asserting oneself—while not the easiest of tasks—is almost always recognized as a positive attribute by others. Remember to speak your truth from your place of compassion and express your sincere desire for a positive outcome and you will succeed in getting what you want and need from others.

Other people cannot read your mind! If your needs are not being met, or you want to express something to a loved one, you must use your shy-strength and make a commitment to show up and be present for yourself by expressing your feelings. Again, using your shy-charm and innate gifts of tact, sensitivity, and good listening skills will serve you well as you begin to practice being more assertive.

Remember to go at your own pace. Be yourself. Don't worry if you are timid about asserting yourself at first, or for some time to come. This may never be an "easy" thing for you to do, but with practice you will become more comfortable and less fearful about standing up for your rights. Those who know and work with you will appreciate your efforts to speak what is on your mind, letting them know how you feel, and what you need from them in order to deepen your relationships and move closer toward what you desire and deserve in your connections with others.

HOW TO ASK FOR WHAT YOU NEED IN RELATIONSHIPS

Many shy people wish that their intimate relationships and friendships weren't so "one-sided," with you doing all the hard work in terms of compromise, compassion, and understanding. If you often feel as if you don't deserve or have the right to be in a bad mood, say no, or take time for yourself, then you probably are not feeling safe enough to express your own needs. This type of dynamic with others can cause resentment and feelings of being taken advantage of and used.

The shy-strong know that they no longer have to feel they are victims. They know that being unable to ask for what one wants from friends and partners eventually leads to an unbalanced relationship with one side doing all the taking and the other doing all the giving.

You may have even come to the point where you feel that being a constant giver of attention and devoted understanding is your role and is what is expected of you. Of course you want to be a loving, giving, and compassionate person, but if this is at the expense of your own happiness then you must challenge yourself to make some changes in the way you relate to others.

If the one-sided relationship is with a spouse or intimate partner, he or she may even have come to *expect* you to not express your feelings. Here are some tips on how to get what you want and need from this type of relationship.

1. Make a list of feelings you would like to express to your loved one. Make another list of needs you feel are not being met which you believe will enhance your intimacy and shared time together.

2. Choose a time to speak when both of you are relaxed and have ample opportunity to spend time together without interruption or distraction.

3. Preface what you are about to say with something positive about your partner and your relationship.

4. Reassure them beforehand that what you are about to say is not a criticism of them, just something you would like to express regarding your feelings.

5. Use "I" statements. For example, "I've noticed that we haven't spent much time together lately." Try not to use "You" to start a discussion: "You are always working and you never

have time for me." "You" statements obviously put the other person on the defensive and they will feel they have done something wrong and are being attacked or criticized.

6. State your feelings with compassion. Risk the vulnerability of speaking from your heart and exposing your feelings, even if they come from a place of insecurity. What you may need is reassurance here, and remember, your partner is not a mind reader.

7. Finally, suggest a joint discussion for a solution: "What can *we* do about this situation so we can love each other more freely?"

Be prepared to hear something unique next. Your partner will probably ask you "What do you want to do?" or "What do you think would be a solution to this problem?" Your partner is now asking about what you want and what you need from the relationship. So give the "problem" some thought before the discussion so you are clear on what you do want and need. Take a risk and try this step-by-step process to ask for what will enhance your relationships with others. This type of dialogue is usually met with great success as long as your partner is open and you approach the talk with a gentle, caring attitude and sincere desire for change.

HOW TO ASK FOR WHAT YOU WANT IN THE WORKPLACE

Standing up for yourself and your rights in your place of work may be even more daunting for some than asserting yourself at home or with friends.

As noted previously, it has been documented that people who are perceived as shy tend to be passed over for promotion and career recognition more than their assertive coworkers. It is unfortunate, but a reality, that certain personality traits are valued in the work environment. But again, you don't have to become someone you are not. You do not have to display aggressive Type-A behavior in order to have a successful career.

You may be more qualified and more knowledgeable than your manager, but if you do not express these attributes in a forthright manner, how is the boss of your company or business to know you would be the perfect person for the job?

The answer lies in confidence. You may be very self-confident that you could do the job better than any other candidate, but if you have trouble convincing others of this confidence, you've lost the opportunity.

Your abilities of being a good listener, being tactful and reserved, and your sense of fairness and self-awareness are all important and vital characteristics of a leader. You already possess what it takes, so it's time to get out of your own way, let go of habitual fear, and use your courage and determination to get what you want.

This is a perfect opportunity for you to practice your Acting as If technique. Even if you are afraid you will fail, or just plain afraid, to assert yourself in your job, you can act as if you are determined and confident in service to your goal of being noticed for the talented and capable employee you know yourself to be.

Speak Up

How many times have you sat in an office meeting where you had some great insights and ideas to offer, but remained silent? A general meeting is a great place to assert your opinion because it is a well-attended forum and you will certainly be noticed. Think about your place of employment. When or where would the most influential and important players hear your knowledge? This is the place where you will start. Office chitchat is fine, and being well liked by your coworkers is important, but if you are actively pursuing a career goal, you must strategize and conserve your energy for the optimal use of your talents. This will also ensure you don't overwhelm yourself in your attempts to assert yourself, which is a new experience for you.

Get Noticed

There are many ways to be noticed at work. Arriving early and staying late is the most often cited, but let's get a bit more creative here. Besides, you are going to need your evenings free for all the new social encounters you are going to be engaging in soon! The best way to get noticed at work is to express thoughtful and insightful input into a difficult account, client, office task, etc. You can probably think of lots of areas that you have great ideas about regarding ways they might be approached and managed better and more efficiently. Employers love a problem-solver. If you have a new and interesting take on how something can operate more smoothly, share it. But share it with someone who can either directly or indirectly advance your standing in the office.

Take Credit Where Credit Is Due

One of the most frustrating experiences at any job, is when someone else, usually someone more aggressive and ambitious than yourself, takes credit for your idea or hard work. Shy people are especially prone to being prey to this unfair treatment. If someone takes advantage of your reticence to assert yourself, as the old saying goes, "don't get mad, get even." Asserting yourself in these situations is not only speaking up against an unfair, although very common work practice, but standing up for yourself will further enhance your goal of getting noticed and being heard and will greatly improve your chance for promotion. And the good news is that whomever felt you were easy prey to further their own ambition will be put on notice that you are no longer someone to be taken advantage of.

Go slowly. Try asserting yourself in simple situations at first. If you have to do an important errand on your lunch break for example, you can assert yourself by politely saying no if someone asks you to go at another, less convenient time for you. Same holds true if you are asked to work through a break. Decide if you are being "used" because you usually do not say "no," or if this is an opportunity for you to begin practicing self-assertiveness.

Also remember your Acting as If technique. In reality you are only acting like most of our coworkers do all the time, who seem to get what they want. Make it a practice of consciously choosing to assert yourself at work at least once a day—even if it is only speaking up in an informal gathering around the coffee machine. As you practice and experience yourself in this new way, the more difficult opportunities, such as asking for a promotion or raise will become less daunting.

REMEMBER TO A.C.T.

Assured

Confident

Trustworthy and tactful

In some deep place within you, once you have stopped the fearful, negative thoughts and replaced them with positive ones, you know you are **A**ssured, **C**onfident, **T**rustworthy, and Tactful at your job. Now it is time to put this knowledge and expertise out in the world where you stand to reap the rewards of your talents.

FREE TO CHOOSE

We've talked about how shy people are often so grateful for any social contact that they tend to not be very choosy when it comes to whom they associate and become friends with. The shy-strong have come to understand that they do not need to fraternize with people who they have nothing in common with, or are hurtful and selfish, or people whom they just plain do not like.

> Make a list of the most important people in your life. Put a "D" for a difficult personality type and a "N.D." for the not difficult ones. Now, mark the people on this list you feel most comfortable being around.

Chances are, if you have experienced shyness, you will have many difficult people in your life in some form or other, whether it is a friend, family member, love interest, or coworker.

All of the personality traits that make you shy-strong— your listening skills, gentleness, compassion, reserve, etc., can actually attract difficult people to you. But this was before you understood these traits to be strengths. Now you can actually be free to choose whether these relationships are serving you in a positive way or leave you feeling badly about yourself.

If an important someone in your life is threatened by, or derides your attempts to change and transform your shyness, you may want to rethink your friendship with him or her. Of course you will give them many opportunities to embrace your commitment to living more fully in the world. But if your tendency to be fearful and timid was the glue which bound you to this person and they are now reluctant to accept your striving for growth, it is time to move on and choose a different type of person to befriend and associate yourself with.

The very attributes that make you shy-strong, are what make you a very loyal friend. And once a shy person makes a friend she tends to do anything in her power, including tolerating less than acceptable behavior, and placing her own needs in the background in order to maintain the friendship.

A true friend will encourage and cheer you on as you move into the world more fully. These are the people you will want to spend more time with as you attempt to solve your shyness. Friends you put an "N.D." next to, if not already your closest friends, will be soon and you will want to put more time and effort into these relationships.

Difficult people generally tend to:

→ Be self-centered and self-absorbed, and even selfish

→ Demand a great deal of your attention and time

→ Put their own needs ahead of others, regardless of the circumstances

→ Be quick to feel and express anger

→ Get easily offended

→ Blame rather than take responsibility for their actions

→ Have unreasonable expectations of what others must do for them

Everyone can be difficult from time to time. But if a person has a difficult nature, you may find yourself "walking on eggshells" around him, afraid of his disapproval or angry outbursts. These folks also tend to have a very hard time with even the slightest confrontation, so the friends they do have are usually much more easygoing and compliant. Having several (or even one!) difficult personality in your social sphere can be exhausting and stressful.

Before you became shy-strong, you may have felt this was just the price you had to pay for friendship. But now you know *you* can choose who you wish to associate and spend time with. The bottom line here is this: If after spending time with a certain friend, you feel drained, depleted, and criticized, i.e., bad about yourself or resentful that the conversation was "all about her," then you would do well to either speak to this person about developing a more balanced friendship, or spend less time with her and more with those whom you feel energized, engaged, and joyful around.

As you meet more people, remember you do not wish to engage in a repetitive pattern of letting other people choose you and then simply going along with them out of your fear of isolation.

Make a list of qualities you would like to have in your friendships. You can also use this list as a reference as you get to know new people. Are they kind, respectful, interested in you? Are they also good listeners, compassionate, and supportive? These are the types of people you will get along with the best and also the ones who will be of greatest assistance to you as you continue on your journey toward greater self-awareness, -acceptance, and -confidence.

CHAPTER NINE: **"**You gain strength, courage and confidence by every experience in which you really stop to look fear in the face. You are able to say to yourself, 'I have lived through this horror. I can take the next thing that comes along.' You must do the thing you think you cannot do.**"**

—Eleanor Roosevelt

The exercises and advice you have read in the previous chapters, along with the step-by-step instructions in Chapter Ten, are aimed at those who feel they are ready to undertake solving issues of shyness that have been hindering their ability to fully and optimistically engage in their lives and achieve their goals. All of the exercises cited are delivered with the confidence that if one is motivated and committed to transforming their shyness from a label of weakness to a trait of strength, they will succeed.

For some however, shyness is a debilitating experience. If you suffer from extreme panic attacks, agoraphobia (which literally means "fear of the marketplace" and usually involves the inability to leave your home, drive a car, take public transportation, have a job, or another experience involving being around other people), or if you have been diagnosed with obsessive compulsive disorder, which also makes it virtually impossible to engage in normal daily activities; then you probably are suffering from what is generally termed "social phobia."

Social phobia is an umbrella description that encompasses behaviors which severely restrict and often forbid one to engage in the outside world. For example, if you have social phobia, you probably do not have a job that requires you to interact with others or work outside your home.

This level of painful isolation from society can only be alleviated through professional treatment. It is probably obvious that if you experience extreme social anxiety, the exercises in this book are not possible for you to undertake at this point in time.

The hopeful news is that there are ways to manage this disorder, if not cure it. You should seek help from a professional who is trained in this particular area. It might be helpful for you to find someone with extensive training in Rational Emotive Behavioral Therapy (REBT).

If the form your social phobia takes is obsessive and compulsive, or if you have a ritual that must be performed repeatedly and leaves little time for going out into the world and also causes you to panic at even the thought of not engaging in this repetitive behavior, you should seek a therapist trained in treating OCD (obsessive compulsive disorder). This therapy will entail a systematic desensitization and involves a gradual process with steps taken very slowly, to help you connect to the outside environment with more comfort and ease.

Experiencing panic attacks or severe anxiety when in the company of other people can also be greatly reduced and cured through treatment with a professional trained in cognitive behavioral therapy with a specific focus on anxiety or panic disorder.

MEDICATION

There are also safe and effective medications, which can be extremely helpful in reducing the physical symptoms anxiety causes, which can be frightening and overwhelming. Some of these medications also target the depression which often accompanies social isolation.

The most common treatment for social phobia and extreme social anxiety is a combination of therapeutic intervention with a therapist specifically trained in this area and medication. Most practitioners will refer you to an M.D. or pharmacologist for a prescription. Be sure to inquire about their experience and expertise in this particular area of social phobia, as well. It is very important that your therapist and medication prescriber are in contact with each other regarding your progress and response to the medication, especially if you experience any side effects. If you find a psychiatrist (who is also an

M.D.) trained in the type of therapy you require, he or she will be able to prescribe medication and you will not need to see any other practitioner.

Medication is mentioned in this chapter because we are dealing with a level of suffering which is intolerable and possibly dangerous since the depression associated with these disorders can be debilitating and can fill one with hopelessness. Please know that this disorder may be related to a chemical imbalance, which is creating and exacerbating your symptoms, and there is absolutely nothing wrong with seeking medical attention for it. If you had diabetes you would not hesitate to take insulin if your doctor told you it would save your life. So it is with extreme panic and depression. There is no shame or weakness in seeking to alleviate your distress with an antidepressant or antianxiety medication.

A word of caution here: If your doctor prescribes any drug in the category known as benzodiazepine, be sure to ask him or her a lot of questions. This class of drugs, like Valium, Xanax, or Atavan, may be fast-acting, but they are highly addictive and can cause memory loss, sedation, and disorientation. If you have a history of alcoholism, or have an addictive personality in other areas of your life, be sure to let your doctor know. There are many other safe alternatives to choose from.

Medication is mentioned in this book because we are talking now about a very extreme condition. The word "shyness" has not been used in this section for a reason. The experience of social phobia is not the same thing as the

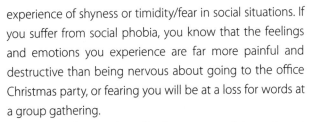

experience of shyness or timidity/fear in social situations. If you suffer from social phobia, you know that the feelings and emotions you experience are far more painful and destructive than being nervous about going to the office Christmas party, or fearing you will be at a loss for words at a group gathering.

Having discussed medication as a possible treatment for this disorder, it must be strongly stressed here that many, many people are able to overcome extreme social phobia through therapy alone. If you choose to take this route, make sure you find a therapist you feel comfortable with. For reasons which are obvious, you will need to trust this person if you are to get better. Since your goal is to address this problem, it is important that you talk to as many therapists as it takes (and you can do this over the telephone if you wish) until you find one that sounds as if he or she is the right person for you to work with.

A great many people like you have successfully dealt with the problem of extreme social anxiety and obsessive-compulsive behaviors. You can become engaged with the world of others if you are willing to take the initial step to seek help. You may even venture out to a group of other people like yourself who may have once despaired of ever having a full and rich life. As you hear their stories of hope and success it will give you the courage you need to ask for and receive the help you need. Please remember, you cannot do this on your own and there is a great deal of help available to you. See Appendices A and B at the back of the book for a helpful list of resources.

putting it all together

CHAPTER TEN: ❝Learn the art of patience. Apply discipline to your thoughts when they become anxious over the outcome of a goal. Impatience breeds anxiety, fear, discouragement and failure. Patience creates confidence, decisiveness and a rational outlook, which eventually leads to success.❞

—Brian Adams

It is now time to use the final step-by-step guide to solving your shyness. In order to be successful in this five-step process, you will need to also keep in mind the techniques you have already learned:

➡ Replace Negative Thoughts with Positive Ones

➡ Thought Stopping

➡ Acting as If

➡ Thought Naming

➡ Naming Your Feelings

➔ Relaxation Techniques

➔ Talk Back (to irrational thoughts and fears)

Before we move on to describing the five steps in detail, there is one more technique you will need to learn and practice: visualization.

MENTAL IMAGERY OR VISUALIZATION

Essentially, visualization is the use of mental imagery to create or change a negative thought into a positive one. With practice, using your mind in this way can manifest extraordinary changes, not only in your attitude and way that you feel about yourself, but also in circumstances in your life. Think of this technique as expanding on Acting as If. In the latter, if you wanted to present yourself in a certain situation with an aura of confidence for example, you would adopt the qualities of a confident person, making them your own—just as an actor would take on a role.

With visualization we are going to add a deeper component to this technique. You are going to actually *see* yourself as that confident person. Think of it as something akin to the difference between *feeling* yourself being the actor, to watching yourself acting out your part on a big screen. The screen, of course, is your mind.

You are already aware that all change requires motivation. Another important component to change is allowing a feeling—a positive and comfortable one—to come into the realm of commitment, motivation, and will to change.

The first step in learning to visualize is relaxation. You will need to do this at a time and in a space where you will not be disturbed for about twenty to thirty minutes.

Some people like to put on soothing instrumental music as they get their minds to quiet down. If you practice meditation, yoga, tai chi, or some other method of formal relaxation, this is a perfect time to spend ten minutes or so engaged in this activity. But this is not absolutely necessary. A quiet, comfortable room will be more than adequate.

If your mind is racing with thoughts of the day you have just had, or worries, imagine putting all of your concerns in the basket of a hot air balloon and untying it and letting your worries and thoughts float away and disappear.

Another image for entering into a relaxed state is to mentally picture yourself by the ocean. As the tide drifts out, imagine your concerns written in the sand, and as the tide comes back in, it will erase your worries. Take your time and remember to breathe slowly, rhythmically, and deeply.

As your mind quiets down and your body relaxes, you are now going to imagine yourself somewhere you feel completely safe, at peace and happy. This may be some-place in nature you have visited, a room in a house in front of a fire, or someplace from your imagination. By a river, a babbling brook, on top of a mountain, in a field of wild flowers, a pine forest, a desert, at the beach? The most important aspect here is the *feeling* of contentment and peace, which arise from being in this place. Again, take your time. Once you have found your "spot" where you feel wonderfully alive and joyful, you are now ready to begin your visualization technique.

Suppose you have an important job interview coming up and you are feeling nervous about it (something all of us would experience nervousness about!). You are going to picture, actually SEE yourself walking into the office building, taking the elevator, entering the office where the interview is to take place, greeting the receptionist, entering the office of the interviewer, sitting down, and beginning the interview. SEE yourself confident, fearless, friendly, and upbeat. Positive. Imagine having an interesting and productive exchange with the interviewer. See them liking you and being pleased with your resume. See yourself talking with expertise and ease. Take your time here. You may even want to bring in some questions you believe you will be asked or want to ask, and SEE yourself answering them in a way that brings a look of satisfaction and respect to the others in the room. In other worlds, SEE yourself acing the interview and getting the job.

If negative thoughts should arise at any time during your visualization session, do your thought stopping (remember the curtain you can use to shut them out?) and move back to seeing yourself in a positive light and with a relaxed and confident frame of mind. Go ahead and visualize this scenario as many times as you like until you get very comfortable with the feeling it generates in you, and you feel you are able to field any question confidently and you are ready for any surprises that may come up. Remember, the most important part of the visualization process is the feeling you experience. You will use this positive energy to connect it to the visualization in order to ensure success.

The Five Steps to Solving Shyness

1. **The situation.** Think of a situation in which you feel fearful, uncomfortable, and timid. (We are going to go through several typical examples using the 5-step program.)

2. **Notice the thoughts.** Look for the negative self-talk that arises from the thought of being in the situation. Notice also the irrational thoughts and the worst-case scenario thoughts.

3. **Do I need to engage in this situation?** Ask yourself if you need to do this. If the answer is yes, then you are going to give the reason WHY and then actually say "SILENCE!" to the fearful thoughts. And replace them with an I Choose statement.

4. **Talk back.** Respond to the negative, self-defeating thoughts with the reasons why the irrational thoughts are not in your best interest and replace them with positive aspects of the situation.

5. **Visualize.** The final step is to replace the negative scenario causing the fearful thoughts with a positive one using visualization and mental imagery.

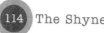

THE FIVE STEPS IN PRACTICE

Example #1: Going to a Party and Meeting New People

Step One: Situation

You have been invited by a friend to come along to a party with him. It is at someone's house that you do not know. You aren't sure if the crowd will be raucous or if it will be a small dinner party, and you don't know if you will know anyone else there besides your friend.

Step Two: Notice the thoughts. What self-defeating and fearful thoughts arise?

Fearful:

→ "No one will talk to me and I'll be too scared to talk to anyone anyway."

→ "I'll have a terrible time and come home depressed."

→ "Being around all those people having fun will just make me feel worse and more lonely."

Irrational:

→ "I'm not going because if people do notice how shy I am, they'll make fun of me and I'll be embarrassed."

→ "If I do go and make a complete fool of myself, I'll humiliate my friend and he'll think I'm a loser who's not worth hanging out with."

Worst-Case Scenario:

→ "I'll lose the one good friend I have and then I'll be totally alone."

Step Three: Do I need to engage in this situation?

"Yes. *Why?* I am trying to solve my shyness and face my fears. I have to go to this party so I can practice being around other people even if it makes me uncomfortable. I need to do this so I can have a full life. I will *SILENCE* the negative thoughts and quit beating myself up about this."

Step Four: Talk back

"I am going to go to this party and try to have fun. I know I can be fun to be with, that's the reason why my friend invited me to come with him. I *choose* to go to this party and I will stay open to possibilities of meeting other people."

Step Five: Visualize

Visualize yourself at the party. You are smiling, friendly, open, and having a good time. *SEE* yourself talking to someone who you feel comfortable with. See yourself relaxed and confident. *FEEL* the feelings that arise with these mental images. You may feel relieved, happy, and proud that others find you interesting. Carry this mental picture with you as you go to the party. When you are there, refer to it. Act as If you are the person you imagined in your visualization. Because you *are* that person.

Example #2: Asking Someone on a Date

Step One: Situation

You are attracted to someone you've met at school, work, the gym, a café, or through a friend. They also seem to share your attraction and have been very friendly to you. You want to get to know him or her better.

Step Two: Notice the thoughts

Fearful:

→ "I'm terrified to ask _____ on a date. What if he/she says no?"

→ " _____ will probably think I'm weird. After all, he/she may think we are just friends."

→ "I better not do this. If _____ says no, I'll be devastated and _____ will never speak to me again, and I'll be too embarrassed to talk to him/her."

Irrational:

→ "Why would this person even want to go out with me? I have nothing to offer and I'll be boring company. Of course, _____ will say no and probably laugh."

Worst-Case Scenario:

→ "If I ask _____ and he/she says no, I'll never be able to ask out another person again and I'll be alone the rest of my life."

Step Three: Do I need to engage in this situation?

"Yes. Why? Because I want to be connected to other people. I want to have love and friendship in my life. If I don't take this risk I will end up alone and that's not how I want to live. I will SILENCE the thoughts that are frightening me about something that could be so wonderful. I will CHOOSE to take a risk to be happy. Nothing ventured, nothing gained."

Step Four: Talk back

"I have been noticing this person for a while now and he/she always seems happy when he/she sees me. I have a lot to offer someone in a relationship. Even if _____ does say NO, I can say something like 'Can't blame me for trying . . .' and ask if we could meet for coffee and be friends. I have the distinct feeling he/she is interested in me or else I wouldn't be doing this in the first place. I'll trust my instincts. I have nothing to lose."

Step Five: Visualize

Visualize going up to the person and making some small talk for a while. See yourself at ease, friendly, and relaxed. See the person smiling back at you, interested in you. Feel how this feels. How it fills you with courage, confidence, and optimism. See yourself asking if he/she would like to have dinner sometime and then see his/her enthusiastic reply of yes! Carry this mental picture of yourself as you go up to the person the next time you see him/her. Act like the person you mentally imagined. That person is actually you."

Example #3: Asserting Yourself in the Workplace

Step One: Situation

A position that entails a promotion, more responsibility, and a substantial salary increase has become available at your place of employment. You know you are very qualified for it.

Step Two: Notice the thoughts

Fearful:

→ "There's no way I would get this job. I am too scared to ask and I wouldn't pass the interview anyway."

→ "Joe wants this job too. He is much more outgoing than me and everyone likes him. He will get it so I shouldn't stick my neck out for failure."

Irrational:

→ "People like me should not be in high positions at this company. I couldn't handle the stress and besides I can't even talk to people. They would never listen to me if I tried to be a manager which is what I would have to do in this position. I don't have the 'people skills' for a job like this."

Worst-Case Scenario:

→ "Even if I did get the job, which I won't, I would be terrible at it and end up getting fired and having no job at all."

Step Three: Do I need to engage in this situation?

"Yes. Why? Because it's a job I am perfect for. I have all the skills required and I want to advance in my career. I will SILENCE the feelings and thoughts of insecurity and I CHOOSE to start believing this is something I can do."

Step Four: Talk back

"I am very qualified for this job promotion. I've paid my dues here and am ready for advancement. I am as knowledgeable as Joe and I look forward to the challenges of being more involved with people I work with. There is a very good possibility I could be hired for this position and I will practice my interview skills beforehand so I am prepared. I have been unhappy for a while in my current position and it is time I made a change. If I don't do this I may regret the loss of a wonderful opportunity, which doesn't come along that often."

Step Five: Visualize

Mentally picture yourself asking for an interview for the job in question. See yourself at the interview conducting yourself with confidence and feeling secure in your expertise and knowledge. See yourself acting friendly, relaxed, and competent. See the interviewer looking at you with interest and respect. See him or her actually becoming more and more convinced that you are the right person for the job, due to the manner in which you are conducting yourself. Feel the feeling as you recognize this in their faces. You feel in command, and esteemed. You are making a very good impression on them and you sense this. Carry this mental picture of yourself into your interview. Act as If you are the person you imagined yourself to be. You wouldn't have been able to imagine this individual if you were not that person already.

Example # 4: Asking for What You Need from Friends
Step One: Situation

A good friend always has very negative things to say about most everything. If it is other friends, choices you make, what you wear, your significant other, or events in the world, she has a harsh and critical opinion that she has no qualms about voicing to you. You want to talk to her about this and ask her to be more considerate of your feelings.

Step Two: Notice the thoughts

Fearful:

→ "I can't say anything to her because she will get mad at me and if I make her angry she won't be my friend anymore. I need all the friends I have and I just have to learn to accept her for who she is."

Irrational:

→ "Maybe she's right. I *am* being too naïve. If what she says bothers me, it is my problem and I should look at my own issues of why she makes me so uncomfortable. It is my fault, not hers."

Worst-Case Scenario:

→ "If I do talk to her she will think I don't like her and she will leave me and tell everyone else not to be friends with me too and I'll be even more alone."

Step Three: Do I need to engage in this situation?

"Yes. Why? Because I always feel terrible after I spend time with her. Her negativity makes me feel inadequate and insecure about myself. It hurts me when she gossips and talks badly about people I like. And her thoughts on my significant other are out of line and unfair. I know her jealousy comes from her own insecurity, but I can't just sit there and say nothing when she is so hurtful. I will SILENCE the fear of standing up to her mean comments and I CHOOSE to act from a place of integrity and truth. I want to feel positive about myself and the world and I need to tell her this. If she decides to not be my friend because I have expressed my feelings to her, then it will be for the best."

Step Four: Talk back

"I am committed to being more positive about myself and my life. I need to surround myself with people who are supportive and kind. I really value my friendship with her, but not at the expense of what I believe in. If she is a really a good friend, she will value what I have to say too and respect me for expressing how I feel. In fact, I am not being a good friend to her if I don't try to help her see that her negativity is unattractive and off-putting to others."

Step Five: Visualize

Imagine yourself sitting down with your friend in a quiet place. See yourself telling her there is something you need to talk to her about. See yourself relaxed, at ease, and friendly. See yourself tell her that when she says negative things about you, it hurts you. Experience how you now feel having just expressed something you have been holding in for some time. Feel yourself relieved, unburdened, and filled with courage for having finally stood up for yourself and spoken the truth. Carry this feeling of confidence with you to your next meeting with your friend. When the time is right, fill yourself with this mental picture of yourself breathing a huge sigh of relief for letting her know that you need her to stop hurting you with her harsh criticism. Act like the person you imagined, full of compassion and integrity and know that is also who you truly are.

Example #5: Asking for What You Need from Family Members

Step One: Situation

You have come to resent the fact that you do everything for your family and you also work at a job. You are expected to cook, clean, help with homework, organize activities on the weekend, be a chauffeur for the kids after school, etc. You have absolutely no time for yourself and this is causing you a great deal of stress.

Step Two: Notice the thoughts

Fearful:

→ "This is my job as a wife and mother. Complaining that I have no time to myself is not only selfish, but will create anger and disharmony in the house."

→ "If I express how I feel to my husband and children they will feel that I do not love them."

→ "I can't ask for what I need because I do not deserve to. I have a wonderful family. I do not want to lose them because of my selfishness."

Irrational:

→ "If I talk to my husband about this, he might leave me since I would be being a bad wife and mother."

Worst-Case Scenario:

→ "It is ridiculous for me to jeopardize my marriage and relationship with my children over something so silly. Besides if I don't do all these things, they will not get done. My children will fail at school and have no social life and friends. My husband will divorce me and I will be alone and devastated."

Step Three: Do I need to engage in this situation?

"Yes. Why? Because I find I am stuffing my feelings of resentment and anger so much it is making me anxious and stressed out. All I am asking for is a little help with some things my family could easily do. I need to do this so I can be an even better mother and wife. I have not been very happy lately and I know the reason why. This can't be good for my family either! I will SILENCE the negative voice that tells me I do not deserve an hour or so a night for myself and I CHOOSE to ask for what I need so I can be more joyful and less resentful."

Step Four: Talk back

"I do not want to feel unhappy and stressed all the time. I want to be able to relax and either read or meditate or go to the gym once in a while. This is important for my personal development and will help me feel better about myself in general. Feeling stressed all the time is an unhealthy way to live. I love my family and they love me. I have never asked them for any help with anything so how could they know this has become such an issue for me? They are not mind readers. It will be good for me to ask for what I need and this will also send a good message to my children that they are also responsible for things around the house that they take for granted. I know my husband loves me and wants me to be happy. He is always saying I do too much anyway. I think he may even be proud of me for speaking up. After all, it may also mean he and I will have more time to spend with each other."

Step Five: Visualize

Mentally picture yourself sitting down with your family to a wonderful dinner (which you've ordered out!). You have a list prepared of ideas for ways in which your family can help out more. You see yourself calm, relaxed, at ease. You tell your family you have been thinking a lot about how the family handles chores, etc., and you want to ask their help in how this can be more balanced. You see yourself telling them you want to feel more available to them, but you don't have a second to spare since it seems you have taken on the entire job of keeping the family running smoothly.

You see your husband holding your hand as you say all this. He is with you 100 percent. You read through your list of what needs to be done that you feel could easily be handled by others. You ask them for help in figuring out this problem. You ask for what you need from them. Who can volunteer to clear the dishes and put them in the dishwasher, walk the dog, make breakfast, cook dinner once a week, help a sibling with homework, vacuum on Saturday morning, etc., etc. You see your family embracing this new idea in a positive way, showing how much they care for and love you. You see a look of surprise and respect come over their faces as they watch you do something you have never done before. Feel the feeling that comes with this. Is it relief? Hope? Happiness? Fill yourself with this feeling and carry it inside you to your talk with your family. Know that feeling less stressed and more relieved, happier and optimistic will be the outcome of your asking for what you need. Act like the confident, loving person you imagined yourself to be in this visualization. She is you.

Example #6: Asking for What You Need from a Coworker

Step One: Situation

You are a member of a team at work. One of your coworkers is constantly asking you to cover for him and do extra work that is his responsibility. You want to say no to him the next time he asks you to finish a report for him.

Step Two: Notice the thoughts

Fearful:

→ "If I say no, the work will not get done and our team will be viewed as irresponsible and poor performers."

→ "Everyone counts on me to be there for them. If I let them down, they will be angry with me and work will become unbearable."

Irrational:

→ "The only reason my team puts up with me is because I always do the extra work so we all look good. If I say no and do not do this for him, I will be ostracized and even more ignored than I already am. Besides, the only time others on my team talk to me is when they want me to do something for them."

Worst-Case Scenario:

➡ "If I say no to him, he just won't do the work and then he will blame it on me somehow and since everyone likes him, he will keep his job and tell the boss it's my fault and I will be the one who gets fired."

Step Three: Do I need to engage in this situation?

"Yes. Why? Because I have been covering for this guy for over a year. I work until eight o'clock most nights and he leaves at five. I bring home work on the weekend and he goes skiing. I am being taken advantage of and I need to start standing up for myself. I will SILENCE the thoughts which tell me I do not deserve to be treated fairly and respectfully. I CHOOSE to say no the next time he asks me to do his work and if I have to I will talk to our supervisor about the situation."

Step Four: Talk back

"I am good at my job. My team respects and likes me. They know I always go the extra mile to help out, but the situation with this one coworker is unacceptable and I have not told anyone about it. I am a team player but enough is enough. If he can't do his own work, he deserves to lose his job. My position is not in jeopardy since my supervisor knows how hard I work and how professional I am. I want to have a life outside of work too. I am not even getting paid for all the overtime I put in doing my own and this other guy's work. I want to learn to be more assertive in my life and this is a perfect opportunity for me to practice those skills. I know I can say this in a way that will not make him angry; but if he does take offense then it is his problem, not mine."

Step Five: Visualize

Mentally picture your coworker coming to up to you on a Friday afternoon and asking if you wouldn't mind finishing up his part of a project due on Monday morning. You see yourself confident, relaxed, and with perhaps a sense of humor as you say, "Sorry, Bill, no can do." You see the look of astonishment on his face. You hear him plead with you, giving you his usual story of how important the upcoming weekend is for him. You feel yourself get stronger in your resolve. You feel powerful and in control. You see yourself tell him not only will you not finish his project, but you are not going to cover for him anymore in the future. And if he can't handle his own workload he should ask someone else to help him or talk to your supervisor.

You see the look of amazement in his eyes since he's never heard you speak this way. You feel great! You are finally standing up for yourself and you see him realize he can no longer have unrealistic expectations of you. You hear him apologize for having leaned on you so much. You see yourself smile at him and say that is all in the past. "From here on out, you are on your own." Carry this feeling of confidence, power, and resolve to work with you. Call upon this mental image the next time he asks an unrealistic "favor" of you. When he inevitably does, Act as If you are the person you imagined yourself to be. In control, determined, and someone not to be taken advantage of. Because that is who you now are.

Example #7: Speaking in Public

Step One: Situation

You must present a talk in front of an audience, promoting a new line your advertising company is launching. Since you are the creator and head of this ad campaign, you are expected to unveil it to the public.

Step Two: Notice the thoughts

Fearful:

→ "There is no way I can do this. I am terrified of speaking in public. I will make a fool of myself and the company will look bad."

→ "If I get up there, I will not remember what I have to say and everyone will be staring at me just standing there, and seeing that I am incompetent."

Irrational:

→ "I have worked so hard on this project. It will fail and the agency will suffer a big loss and be extremely disappointed in me if I fail, which I know I will."

Worst-Case Scenario:

→ "If I do go up there and do not succeed in promoting this line, I will never be put in charge of a large account again and word will get out that I cannot do my job, so when they let me go, no one else will take a chance on me."

Step Three: Do I need to engage in this situation?

"Yes. Why? Because this is part of my job. I am the creative director of this line and it is my pride and joy. I know I have to get over this fear of speaking in public if I am to advance in my career and be given other great opportunities like this one. I will SILENCE the self-defeating thoughts that tell me I will be a failure and I CHOOSE to do the best I can at Acting as If I am confident, even though I will probably feel nervous."

Step Four: Talk back

"I know this project inside and out. No one else would be able to speak about it as passionately as I can. I believe this is my best work and I have a responsibility to show up for all the time and effort I have put into it. I do not want to regret not seeing this thing through to the end. If I did get someone else to do the presentation who isn't able to answer questions from the audience, then the work will not be seen in its most positive light. I would never forgive myself if it did not sell because I was too afraid to get up there and handle the pressure. I am a professional and I am completely prepared for any and all questions that might arise. If I can do this, it will also position me for a big advance in my career, which is what I want and have spent years working toward."

Step Five: Visualize

Mentally picture the presentation of the line being shown on a video screen. You are introduced as the creator and an appreciative audience applauds as you walk out. You may feel a bit nervous, but you will choose to transform this feeling into excitement and energy. You feel confident, in control, and very prepared. You see yourself walking over to the microphone and beginning to speak. You are amazed at how easy it is to talk about something you have lived and breathed for three years. You feel more at ease as you begin talking about the qualities and benefits of this product. This is something you believe in and you see yourself conveying this genuineness to the audience. You see yourself acting natural, speaking in a confident tone. Feel the feeling of being in control, of being knowledgeable and prepared.

See yourself finishing up your presentation and asking for questions. Feel how easy it is for you to call upon people and answer their queries intelligently. Now, see yourself standing with your team after the presentation. Your fellow workers are congratulating you on a job well done. You feel proud and of course relieved, but filled with satisfaction and peace of mind that you were able to accomplish something you never dreamed you were capable of. Carry this feeling of confidence, pride, and determination with you the day of your presentation. Mentally review this visualization. Fill yourself up with the feelings you felt as you Act as If you are the person you imagined, because there is no doubt about it: That person is you.

FINAL NOTE

There are many books, groups, and Internet sites that offer assistance to those engaging in the journey of becoming shy-strong. In Appendix B at the end of this book, you'll find some of the most popular Web sites, and you will find a detailed description of what you will encounter if you choose to further enlarge your social network and connections through these sites. Note that all of these resources are specifically aimed at "overcoming" shyness. *The Shyness Solution* posits that shyness is a personality trait with a lot of wonderful qualities, which must be integrated and acknowledged, not "overcome" or "conquered." As you look through the resources, remember to keep in mind that you are not going to go back to a negative view of yourself as terminally "shy," but bring with you to any of these resources that might interest you the view that you are engaged in transforming yourself. You may even find that you will look at the resource material in a completely new way!

appendix a

List of Resources

Shyness Surveys

These questionnaires are sponsored by the Shyness Institute in Palo Alto, California, and may be useful to you if you are interested in further gauging your level of shyness and comfort level around others.

Can I Count on You? A questionnaire to help you answer the question: "Can I count on this person to be there for me emotionally in difficult times?"

The Henderson Zimbardo Shyness Questionnaire. This is part of the research being done on shyness at the Shyness Institute. They assure that all information is confidential.

Books (* denotes highly recommended)

The following lists of books were recommended by members of *alt.support.shyness*, which is an excellent site detailed in Appendix B.

Shyness: A Bold New Approach (2000) by Bernardo Carducci

The Shy Life: A Psychologist Examines the Nature of Shyness and Offers Steps Towards Finding Your Comfort Zone (1998) by Bernardo Carducci

Shyness: A Bold New Approach: Managing Your Shyness at Work, Making Small Talk, Navigating Social Situations, Parenting a Shy Child (2000) by Bernardo Carducci

Feel the Fear and Do It Anyway (1992) by Susan Jeffers

The Highly Sensitive Person (1996) by Elaine Aron: "Possessing this trait can make life challenging at times," says the author, but she says that being sensitive is not a psychological disorder or a personality flaw to get rid of. The sensitivity trait is merely a part of an individual's personality. This book is less self-help and more self-acceptance.

The Shyness Workbook (1979) by Phil Zimbardo

Beyond Shyness: How to Conquer Social Anxieties (1993) by Jonathan Berent and Amy Lemley

Overcoming Shyness (1993) by Blaine Smith

The Hidden Face of Shyness: Understanding and Overcoming Social Anxiety (1996) by Franklin Schneier and Lawrence Welkowitz

Social Phobia: From Shyness to Stage Fright (1995) by John Marshall

Conquer Shyness: Understand Your Shyness and Banish It Forever (1997) by Frank Bruno

Shyness: Your Questions Answered (1998) by Lynne Crawford and Linda Taylor

The Shy Guy's Guide to Dating (1998) by Barry Dutter

Talking With Confidence for the Painfully Shy (1997) by Don Gabor

How to Start a Conversation and Make Friends by Don Gabor

Conversationally Speaking by Alan Garner

Overcoming Shyness and Social Phobia: A Step-by-Step Guide (1998) by Ronald M. Rapee

Diagonally-Parked in a Parallel Universe by Signe A. Dayhoff

BOOKS FOR CHILDREN

I'm Shy; A Bashful Little Pop-Up Book (1993) by David Carter

The Blushful Hippopotamus (1996) by Chris Rashcka

The Shy Little Kitten (1997) by Schurr

How Kids Make Friends: Secrets for Making Lots of Friends, No Matter How Shy You Are (1997) by Lonnie Michelle

It's OK to Be Shy (1998) by Mitch Golant

Let's Talk About Being Shy (1997) by Marianne Johnston

MISCELLANEOUS

Shyness is a ten-minute animated film that uses humor to reconstruct the Frankenstein story to show how to overcome shyness. It's available through Bullfrog Films, P.O. Box 149, Oley, PA 19547. Here are some comments from viewers:

→ "Great for children and adolescents, it operates on another level for adults . . . the concrete suggestions given to overcome shyness are known to be effective, perhaps more so for grown ups."

→ "A terrific resource for library and community groups or educational programs."

TREATMENT CENTERS AND PROGRAMS

American Psychological Association. Gives referrals for psychologists in your area who deal with issues of shyness and social phobia. Telephone: 1-800-964-2000.

Center for Shyness and Social Therapy. Jonathan Berent, M.S.W. Berent Associates. Address: 17 Maple Drive, Greatneck, New York. Telephone: 1-800-248-2034.

appendix b

Internet Resources

Shy and Free (www.shyandfree.com)

This site is a well-organized, insightful, and award-winning Web site created by Kevin Rhea, which has sections with titles like "Life After Shyness," which suits our purposes just fine. There is a "process" section that offers some wonderful ideas regarding how to deepen your commitment to transforming shyness into strength and confidence. Another section on "secrets" of shyness is essentially about how to create more of a balance in your life. This section includes ways to achieve your goals, stories from other people who are engaged in a dialogue with the shy parts of themselves, and a very good list of other resources including short reviews of other books and references on shyness. "The Principles of Shyness" as Mr. Rhea has defined them, are worth repeating here since many of them reinforce the exercises you have been working on in this book. They are also positive statements, and will give you a good idea of the kind of approach you will want to look for as you search out more information.

Principles that Transform Shyness (from the Shy and Free Web site)

1. You are not like everyone else.

2. You are more than your shyness.

3. Shyness is serving you.

4. You are responsible for your actions, not your feelings.

5. When you feel safe, you do not feel shy.

6. Balancing the Mind, Body, and Spirit leads to transformation.

7. Success is available every moment.

8. Shyness is an inner guide.

9. The answer is within.

10. Trust the universe instead of attempting control.

11. Not everyone was meant to be your friend or partner.

12. Obsession is a sign telling you to let go.

13. Your beliefs create your reality.

14. Nothing is wrong with you.

15. You are loved for your flaws.

16. You are shy because you have important lessons ahead.

17. Lessons will be repeated until you understand and learn.

18. Extraordinary effort is required.

19. Now is the best time to begin your transformation.

20. Those who know you as shy limit your freedom.

21. Addictions deplete your transformative energy.

22. Being shy is not better or worse than being outgoing.

23. Shyness exists within, not without.

24. You are as important as anyone else.

25. Your past was pre-destined, your future is not.

26. Manipulation will not get you what you really want.

27. Help others, help self.

Highly Sensitive People (www.sensitiveperson.com)

This interesting Web site posits that shyness is another term for "spiritual introvert." It focuses a lot on "sensitivity, intuitive feelings, and dreams." This site is worth a look if you want to find a "sensitive pal or soul-mate." They also have a message board where you can communicate with others in an open forum. This Web site is quite specific in both its target audience and content. If it isn't for you, try some other ones.

The Social Fitness Forum (veryshy@ucsd.edu)

This is another online bulletin board for discussions about "social fitness: sharing, strategies, resources, and networking."

Beating Shyness in the Business World
(www.shakeyourshyness.com)

This Web site offers more tips and strategies for dealing with timidity in the workplace. It can also boost your morale with such things as detailed discussions of shy celebrities (both past and present). It also offers advice for parents of a shy child, with some insightful and specific information on how to help children who experience shyness in the classroom. As with most of these resources, this one also offers a link to other Web sites on shyness.

Shyness.Com (www.shyness.com)

This Internet site offers a more clinical and academic explanation of shyness and its treatment. The section entitled "Encyclopedia of Mental Health . . . Shyness" by Lynne Henderson and Phillip Zimbardo is really written for professionals, but if you feel you want a more intellectual (and educational) challenge, go ahead and take a look at the "Research and Study" section, which offers different views of shyness and includes such interesting studies as explorations of cultural differences in determining shy behavioral traits, for example.

Alternative Shyness Support
(www.alt.support.shyness.com)

This Internet resource is a one-stop shopping mall for all things shy. From understanding the origins of shyness to discussions of how "non-shy" people regard the shy, to answering questions such as "Is shyness a form of low self-esteem or selfishness"? This Web site offers a lot of great

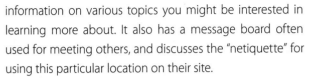

information on various topics you might be interested in learning more about. It also has a message board often used for meeting others, and discusses the "netiquette" for using this particular location on their site.

This particular resource can be especially helpful when used in conjunction with what you have learned in *The Shyness Solution*, because it takes a similar, pro-action approach to solving shyness.

This is probably the best Web site on the Internet and everything discussed in other sites mentioned previously will be found here as well. Especially helpful is the section on books, which is divided into categories and will be very useful should you decide to take your learning even further and make additional changes to your life such as job hunting, finding love, assertiveness, and conversational techniques.

Rational Emotive Behavioral Therapy (www.rebt.org)

Along with reading the book, *How to Stubbornly Refuse to Make Yourself Miserable About Anything—Yes, Anything!* by Albert Ellis, Ph.D., who is also the founder of Rational Emotive Behavior Therapy (REBT); you may wish to visit this Web site which is devoted to his philosophy. Many of the exercises in *The Shyness Solution* draw from the theories developed by Dr. Ellis, which essentially state that our thoughts create our feelings. If we can change the thoughts, we can change the feelings they cause.

Shy Kids (www.Shykids.com)

This is a wonderful resource/Web site for children, tweens, teens, parents, and teachers designed for young people who experience shyness. The unique quality of this site is described in their mission statement: "We are staffed by former shy kids, blossoming shy kids, and parents helping them along the way." It is an excellent place to start for a youngster experiencing the painful social isolation from peers a shy child sometimes endures in the school environment. It has a positive, upbeat style that will appeal to children and teens and the 'Chit-chat' section has some terrific suggestions for conversation starters in awkward social situations.

Resources for Shy People (www.base.com)

This Web site offers testimonials from others: "I used to be incredibly shy. In the last few years I have really focused on attempting to overcome my shyness. I am still somewhat shy today, but far less so than I used to be." It also has a very good compilation of articles, advice, newsgroups, dating connections, e-mail lists, and books. It also lists shyness clinics, classes, and counseling services available.

The American Psychological Association Help Center (www.apahelpcenter.org)

This is a great site that offers advice and information and different articles on shyness. It is also a place where you can find a psychologist in your area who is trained in treating social phobia.

Social Anxiety Center (www.socialanxiety.com)

This is a Web site managed by Jonathan Berent, who along with Amy Lemley, is the author of *Beyond Shyness: How to*

Conquer Social Anxieties. One of the features of this site which distinguishes it from others is that it addresses learning disabilities.

Craig's Shyness Resource Page (www.csbruce.com)

This is one of the more popular sites on the Internet. In the first line of the Web site it says "You are not Alone," which informs the direction Mr. Bruce takes. You will find essays, articles, newsgroups, links to other sites, topics of interest such as public speaking and leadership (and gives the resource of the Toastmasters Club, an informal public speaking arena, where one may practice the skills newly acquired here). This site has an offbeat sense of humor and rather irreverent tone, so you may not wish to visit it if you are easily offended by titles like "Involuntary Celibacy" or "It's a Borderline Personality World."

Planet Psych.com (www.planetpsych.com)

Describes itself as "A World of Information." A psychology-based Web site, you will need to type in "shyness" in the search bar. You will find a directory of therapists, sections on self-help (which has a wonderful chapter on relaxation techniques), Psychology 101 (which discusses specific disorders relating to shyness in layperson terms), an interactive section with quizzes, tests, and news forums, and a bookstore.

> Please note: the author and publisher of *The Shyness Solution* do not assume responsibility for any material or content which may be transmitted via any of the sites on the Internet. These Web sites are mentioned because they are the most popular and most visited locations that deal with issues of shyness.

appendix c

Glossary of Terms

Acting as If: A technique used to adopt a role or personality trait which one wishes to present themselves as possessing.

Aggression: Hostile or destructive behavior.

Agoraphobia: An abnormal fear of public places or people.

All or Nothing expectations: The belief that unless one is perfect, one is a failure.

Anxiety disorder: A nervous condition that creates extreme mental and physical discomfort in certain situations.

Assertiveness: Stating and expressing one's rights in a positive way.

Attributes: Inherent characteristics of a person.

Autonomy: The capacity to manage one's affairs and make decisions for oneself.

Body language: The bodily gestures, postures, and facial expressions by which one communicates nonverbally with others.

Confidence: A feeling of self-assurance and quality of being certain about oneself.

Conversation: A spoken exchange of thoughts, opinions, and feelings.

Ego: The part of the psyche that is conscious and controls thought and behavior.

Empathy: Identification with and understanding another's thoughts, feelings, and motivations.

Extrovert: An individual primarily interested in the environment and others as opposed to the self.

Gentility: The quality of being considerate and kind in one's nature.

Humility: A quality which includes lack of vanity and self-importance.

Insecurity: Feelings of self-doubt and uncertainty.

Intimacy: The ability to have close friends and relationships and the capacity for allowing others close to oneself.

Introvert: One whose thoughts and feelings are directed toward the self.

Irrational thinking: Thoughts which lack mental clarity, reason, and sound judgment.

Isolation: To set oneself apart or cut oneself off from others.

Modesty: Behavior free from pretension or ostentation.

Name That Feeling: The technique of mindful noticing of feelings and making a cognitive connection to the experience.

Nature vs. nurture: Argument for whether one is born with a certain personality trait or it is created by their environment.

Obsessive compulsive disorder: A thought disorder that includes uncontrollable urges to perform repetitive behaviors.

Panic disorder: A psychological disorder that affects one by seizing them with sudden, overpowering terror.

Passion: Boundless enthusiasm for something one loves and has a deep interest in.

Perfectionism: The tendency to be displeased with anything that does not meet extremely high standards, and which are often unattainable.

REBT: Rational Emotive Behavioral Therapy. A type of therapy which posits that thoughts can create feelings. If the thought can be changed, the feeling will change also.

Relaxation techniques: The use of specific mental imagery and exercises which help quiet the racing thoughts of the mind, so it is more susceptible to positive suggestion.

Reserve: Keeping one's feelings, thoughts, and affairs to oneself in an effort to refrain from harmful gossip.

Security: Freedom from doubt, anxiety, or fear.

Self-consciousness: Socially ill at ease and excessively aware of one's appearance or manner.

Self-esteem: The pride one takes in oneself and one's achievements. Self-respect.

Sensitivity: Sympathetic insight into others' feelings.

Shame: A painful emotion caused by a sense of unworthiness.

Social phobia: A severe and debilitating fear of people and public places which can limit one's life.

Social withdrawal: The tendency to refrain from engaging in social situations involving other people.

Spiritual practice: Techniques which further enhance one's self-awareness and peace of mind.

Shy-strength: Transformation of a liability into an asset through a change in thinking.

Tact: The ability to speak or act without offending another.

Talk Back: Challenging negative thinking with positive thought replacement.

Thought Stopping: Using mental imagery to cease certain destructive, unhealthy thoughts.

Transformation: A marked change in appearance or character that is positive and life-affirming.

Trust: Firm belief in the ability, character, and integrity of another person or of oneself.

Type-A Personality: A characteristic or quality marked by ambition, drive, and often aggression.

Visualization: Forming a mental image of a situation, place, or feeling.

index

A.C.T. (Assured, Confident, Trustworthy), 99
Acting as If, 34, 38–41. *See also* Visualization
Affirmations, 24, 27, 31, 32
Assertiveness, 89–93
Belief systems, 18–20, 23
Benefits, of shyness, 21–32, 33–41. *See also* Shy-strength
  comfort with self, 15–16
  current societal views and, 21–22
  gentleness, 23–24
  insecurity, 27–31
  listing, 18
  modesty, 24–25
  sensitivity, 31–32
  tact/reserve, 25–27
Body language, 55–56
Case studies
  Acting as If, 40–41
  asking for what you need, 120–28
  childhood environment, 14
  meeting people, 77–79, 114–16
  naming feelings, 60–61
  parties, 26–27, 77–79, 114–16
  public speaking, 40–41, 129–31
  workplace, 118–20, 126–28, 129–31
Change
  belief systems and, 18–20, 23
  requirements for, 18
  resistance to, 20
  to shy-strength, 33–36
Conversation, 50–56
  art of, 50–53
  body language and, 55–56
  developing skills/knowledge, 51–54
  at parties, 80
Dating. *See* Love shy
Extroverts, 85–102
  asking for what you need among, 93–99
  assertiveness, aggression and, 89–93

challenges around, 85–89
choosing friends/associates among, 99–102
Eye contact, 55–56
Family, asking for needs from, 122–25
Fear. *See also* Insecurity
  confronting, 23, 47–50, 59–61. *See also* Solving shyness examples
  as friend, 21
  as illusion, 33
  of intimacy, 15, 16
  Naming a Feeling and, 59–61
  replacing with strength, 23, 33–36
  universality of, 23–24
F.I.B. (fear, irrationality, bad habit), 47–50
Five-step process. *See* Solving shyness examples
Friends
  asking for what you need from, 120–22
  bringing along to party, 79
  choosing, 99–102
  meeting people through, 68–69
Fun shy, 43–56. *See also* Conversation; Self-consciousness
  body language and, 55–56
  defined, 44
  Thought Naming and, 45–50
Gentleness, 23–24
Glossary of terms, 144–48
Habits
  bad, confronting, 47–50
  changing, 18
  of shyness, 17–18
Insecurity, 27–31
  self-esteem and, 27–28
  as teacher, 28–29, 31
  Thought Stopping and, 29–30, 36–38
  universality of, 23–24, 59
Internet dating, 71–73
Internet resources, 137–43

148

Intimacy. *See also* Love shy
    fear of, 15, 16
    motivating development of,
        15–16
Irrationality, 47–50. *See also* Solving
    shyness examples
Love shy, 58–73
    asking for what you need,
        93–95
    being yourself and, 62–63
    bookstores as meeting places,
        66–67
    challenges, 57–59
    dating tips, 63–64, 116–18
    friends/networking and, 68–69
    Internet dating and, 71–73
    joining groups and, 70
    meeting people and, 64–73,
        77–79, 114–16
    Naming a Feeling and, 59–61
    spiritual practices and, 67–68
    volunteering and, 68
    workout meeting places, 64–66
    workshops/classes and, 69–70
Medication, 105–7
Meditation, 45–46
Modesty, 24–25
Naming a Feeling, 59–61
Negative thought replacement. *See*
    Thought Stopping
Negativity, confronting, 47–50
Parties, 75–83
    bringing friends along, 79
    case studies, 26–27, 77–79,
        114–16
    conversation, 80
    gauging comfort level, 81–83
    hanging around food, 79–80
    "life of" defined, 76
    observing others, 81
Past influences, 13–20
    case study, 14
    childhood influences, 14–16
    documenting/identifying,
        16–17
Perfectionism, 28
Posture, 56
Rating shyness level, 2–11
Resources, 133–43

Security/safety, 19
Self-consciousness. *See also* Fun shy
    being yourself and, 62–63
    described, 44
    Thought Naming and, 45–50
Self-esteem, insecurity and, 27–28
Sensitivity, 31–32
Shy-strength. *See also* Benefits, of
    shyness
    charming qualities, 33–36
    defined, 19
    transforming shyness to, 33–36
Social phobias, 34, 104
Solitude, as strength, 15–16, 24
Solving shyness examples, 114–31
    asking for what you need,
        120–28
    asking someone on a date,
        116–17
    going to party/meeting people,
        114–15
    public speaking, 129–31
    steps overview, 113
    workplace situations, 118–20,
        126–28, 129–31
Strengths. *See* Benefits, of shyness;
    Shy-strength
Tact/reserve, 25–27
Talk back (to irrational thoughts/
    fears), 113, 115, 117, 119, 121–
    22, 124, 127–28, 130
Therapy, 17, 104–5, 136
Thought Naming, 45–50. *See also*
    Solving shyness examples
    confronting negativity, 47–50
    F.I.B. and, 47–50
    meditation and, 45–46
Thought Stopping, 29–30, 36–38,
    61. *See also* Solving shyness
    examples
Trust, 15
Visualization, 110–13, 115–16,
    117–18, 119–20, 122, 125, 128,
    130–31
Workplace situations, 95–99,
    118–20, 126–28